Beyond *Common Worship*

Beyond *Common Worship*

Anglican Identity and Liturgical Diversity

Mark Earey

scm press

© Mark Earey 2013

Published in 2013 by SCM Press
Editorial office
3rd Floor,
Invicta House
108–114 Golden Lane,
London
EC1Y 0TG, UK

SCM Press is an imprint of Hymns Ancient & Modern Ltd
(a registered charity)
13A Hellesdon Park Road
Norwich NR6 5DR, UK

www.scmpress.co.uk

The sample canons in Appendix 2 are from *The Canons of the Church
of England*, 7th edition, Church House Publishing, 2012
© The Archbishops' Council

British Library Cataloguing in Publication data

A catalogue record for this book is available
from the British Library

978-0-334-04739-1

Typeset by Manila Typesetting Company
Printed and bound by
CPI Group (UK) Ltd, Croydon

Contents

Acknowledgements

I would like to thank all those who have rung or emailed me (or simply collared me in a class or at a conference or meeting) over the last 16 years and asked a question about *Common Worship*. It is those questions which first helped me to see the need for some simple answers in the short term and for some creative thinking in the longer term.

More recently, I have had the opportunity to try out some of the ideas in this book on unsuspecting students, both at The Queen's Foundation and at St John's College, Nottingham. Further afield, I would like to thank ordinands and clergy in other contexts, including the students of the Southern North West Training Partnership in January 2012, attendees of a Praxis North West day in June 2012, and the clergy of Coventry Diocese at their Bishop's study day in November 2012. My colleagues on the Church of England Liturgical Commission were kind enough to give me time on the agenda of our meeting in January 2013 and indulged me in a discussion of the issues raised in this book. I should make clear that although I have gained hugely from their insights, I am writing here in a personal capacity, and the ideas put forward in this book should not be taken as representative of any 'official' view of the Liturgical Commission.

In particular, I would like to thank the Principal of St John's College, Durham, and the members of the planning committee of the Michael Vasey Lecture, who were kind enough to invite me to give the annual Vasey lecture in March 2012. That invitation was the initial spur which prompted me to put my ideas into some sort of coherent shape.

ACKNOWLEDGEMENTS

To all those who spoke to me individually at any of these events or who asked key questions in plenary, which helped to focus my thinking or which challenged my proposals, I offer grateful thanks. You may well see echoes of your questions in what follows (in which case, many thanks) or you may feel that I have misrepresented the point you were making (in which case, sincere apologies). In all cases, I accept that no one but me is responsible for any weaknesses that remain.

As the material took a more finalized shape, I am grateful to those who read initial drafts and provided feedback: Alison Earey, James Hill, Jonny Baker, John Leach and David Green. Finally, I would like to thank Dr Natalie Watson of SCM Press, who has encouraged me to bring the book to publication and given advice and guidance along the way. My wife Alison and daughter Hannah have been patient, as ever, and encouraged me throughout the process. To them I offer more thanks than I can say.

Abbreviations Used in this Book

ASB   *The Alternative Service Book 1980*

ASW   A Service of the Word

BCP   *The Book of Common Prayer*

CW   *Common Worship* (in its generic sense – not referring
       to a particular volume)

MWB   *Methodist Worship Book 1999*

Introduction

This is an odd book for me to find myself writing. For most of the last 16 years I have been closely involved in one way or another with the production of *Common Worship* services, and with helping people to know how to use them. In short, I have a lot invested in *Common Worship*. To write a book which might seem, at first sight, to be critical of that work is odd. However, as I hope will become apparent, the book is not meant to be critical of the material in *Common Worship* itself, but an invitation to ask ourselves where the Church of England might head next, building on what we have learnt through the use of *Common Worship*.

Questions, questions

From 1997 to 2002 I was National Education Officer for Praxis, a Church of England organization for liturgical renewal and education.

> **Praxis**
>
> Praxis was formed in 1990, sponsored (but not paid for) by the Liturgical Commission and two Church of England liturgical organizations, the Alcuin Club (a society promoting sound liturgical scholarship, particularly with reference to the Anglican Communion) and the Group for Renewal of Worship (the group behind the Grove Worship series). The aim was to bring together those from different traditions

from within the Church of England who shared a concern for improving the practice of worship. In the process, it became seen as a sort of 'semi-official' education and formation arm of the Liturgical Commission. For more about Praxis, visit www.praxisworship.org.

During this time, I was an observer on the Liturgical Commission and a member of the Education and Formation subcommittee of the Liturgical Publishing Group. I wrote leaflets helping to prepare the Church of England for the new services, edited a series of books on 'Using *Common Worship*' and produced a range of Praxis training packs designed to help people at parish level to introduce the services to their PCCs and congregations and to use them with understanding.

At this point, the Church of England had no national liturgy officer, and I regularly got emails and phone calls asking practical questions about *Common Worship* and how to use it. I thought that the questions would die down as the new services got embedded into the Church's life, but in my later experience as a parish priest they still came. In my current work as Liturgy Tutor at The Queen's Foundation in Birmingham, I still get the questions – and not just from ordinands discovering *Common Worship* for the first time, but from experienced parish clergy who have been working with it for a while.

It is this experience of seeing how *Common Worship* is actually working out which has prompted this book. Like most people, I have my own views about which bits of *Common Worship* work well and which need a bit of work, but overall I still strongly believe that the *Common Worship* 'project' was and is good, and that the material builds well on what had gone before it in Series One, Two and Three, and *The Alternative Service Book 1980*. Though *Common Worship* may have its faults, it is not primarily the material which is a problem, but the system within which the material sits. It has become my conviction that this system needs to change, and that we would do well to approach that change proactively and intentionally rather than have it forced upon us piecemeal.

Reflections on *Common Worship* so far

Thus far there have been few books which have reflected on *Common Worship* in any depth. In 2011, Nicholas Papadopulos edited *God's Transforming Work: Celebrating Ten Years of Common Worship* (London: SPCK, 2011). The ten years in the title should be understood flexibly – the obvious year to mark would be 2000, because that was when the authorization of *The Alternative Service Book 1980* ran out and *Common Worship* had to take over, but the first part of *Common Worship* (the Calendar, Lectionary and Collects) came out in 1997, before it was even called *Common Worship*, and many other parts of *Common Worship* came out after 2000.

As the subtitle suggests, this was a volume celebrating the achievement and impact of *Common Worship*. It contains essays primarily by people involved in and around the production of the services, who note its impact in a range of areas and, in a few cases, make some suggestion for future changes.

There have been some brief attempts to analyse the process and history which led from ASB 1980 to *Common Worship*, including Michael Perham's chapter 'Liturgical Revision 1981–2000' in Paul Bradshaw (ed.), *Companion to Common Worship Vol. 1* (London: SPCK, 2001) and David Hebblethwaite's reflections as secretary to the Liturgical Commission in *Liturgical Revision in the Church of England 1984–2004: The Working of the Liturgical Commission,* Alcuin/GROW Joint Liturgical Studies 57 (Cambridge: Grove Books, 2004). These give good background information and can help us to understand how we ended up with what we have.

What is still to come is both a sustained critique of the material itself (which might help us to see what is needed next) and some exploration of the bigger-picture question as to whether the whole direction of liturgical revision has been right. It is this second, bigger-picture, question which I explore here.

There is, of course, another possible strategy for responding to *Common Worship*, and that is to say that the whole process of liturgical revision has been flawed from start to finish, and that much of the decline in churchgoing has been because of confusion and a decline in standards since the widespread abandonment of *The Book of Common Prayer*. I have stated this in strong terms, but there are those who feel that the surest way to move on from *Common Worship* is to encourage a return to the Prayer Book, to stability in form and beauty in language – at least, as perceived by some.

While I value the Prayer Book and all that it stands for, I don't think that is the answer. Liturgical renewal and reform may not have 'saved' the Church, but neither has it caused decline in the Church. That decline (if you see it like that) has been the result of a range of factors. The only true measure of the impact of liturgical revision in that mix would be if we could compare the state of the Church *with* liturgical revision, with the situation if we had *not* had liturgical revision. We do not have access to that comparison, but if we did we might find that the decline would have been even worse had we not had liturgical variety, services in modern English, and so on. So for now, I shall assume that there is no going back, only a moving forward with a more diverse pattern, even though the Prayer Book still has a key place within that diversity. The rest of this book will explore what that movement forward might look like.

I

What is the Problem?

What's wrong with *Common Worship*? In one sense, nothing. *Common Worship* has been a great success at fostering both variety and flexibility in Church of England worship. Of course, there are some things that can be improved about the texts, and that is an ongoing project. The production of new Eucharistic Prayers for use with children is one example of this; the current work to produce alternative texts for some parts of the initiation services is another. The fact that after the *Common Worship* Collects were agreed and published, a further set of additional Collects were deemed to be necessary is a third.

However, it is not the texts of *Common Worship* that this book is about, and I want to be clear that overall I think CW has been a great gain for the Church of England. It may not be perfect, but I think it has been the best it could have been, given the context in which it has been developed and has to work.

I am looking 'beyond *Common Worship*' not in the sense of 'What new services or resources do we need next?', but in the sense of 'What has the CW *approach* done to our worship, and what is it doing to it now?' Most importantly, I want to ask what that approach will do to worship in the future, especially in an era of missional thinking, fresh expressions of church, new monasticism, pioneering approaches, artistic creativity, so-called 'alt.worship' and so on.

In this book, then, I am using CW to stand for the whole 'project' of liturgical revision and the production of texts which are alternative to *The Book of Common Prayer* (BCP), a project which has been active since the mid-1960s and had been contemplated for even longer. In some ways, to call this a CW approach is misleading, because CW is simply the inheritor, or latest incarnation, of this post-1960s project. This book could have been called *Beyond Alternative Services*, because what I am questioning is the particular way the Church of England, since 1965, has held the balance between local decision-making and shared (or 'common') forms of worship.

This will involve us considering what makes worship truly 'Anglican' and how we can ensure good decisions at local level. It is about the tension between common forms and local needs, between a catholic approach (in the sense of connected with the wider Church, and transcending local cultures) and an inculturated approach, which takes those cultures not only seriously, but as a key starting point in understanding what will make 'good' worship.

A hybrid liturgy?

The desire both to provide variety and flexibility and to preserve some commonality has produced a hybrid liturgy which is neither common enough for some, nor flexible enough for others. Some of this problem is as much about changes in the Church more widely as it is about the liturgy itself.

To use a computer analogy, *Common Worship* has ended up feeling like a sophisticated piece of software being run on a computer whose basic operating system is now many years out of date and was built for running very different programs. The operating system has been updated and 'patched', and there are various 'work arounds' to help people to do what they want or need the software to do, but the result feels clunky and difficult, and the whole thing frequently crashes, being unable to do what is being asked of it.

The Church of England's worship 'operating system' consists of its canon law. It was designed for a situation in which there was one service book – *The Book of Common Prayer*. It is designed to protect and preserve that prayer book, but has been 'patched' by the Prayer Book (Alternative and Other Services) Measure 1965 and the later Worship and Doctrine Measure of 1974 to allow for authorized alternatives to be used alongside it. Those 'patches' have been constantly updated to try to provide ways of allowing greater flexibility, such as the production of 'commended' services to use alongside authorized alternatives, and the provision of authorized outline structures to use alongside fully worked-out orders of service. The result is that you can 'work around' the operating system, but the ways of doing this are not always (indeed, are rarely) intuitive to users.

What is needed is a new streamlined operating system, designed to allow the software to work at its most efficient. The software program needs to be able to 'just work', rather than drawing time, energy and attention to itself.

What this book offers is not ideas about new 'software' to supersede *Common Worship*, but a new operating system – that is, a new way of structuring the Church of England's way of allowing for flexibility while also keeping a sense of Anglican commonality. In order to do this, we will first look at some of the problems or difficulties raised by users of *Common Worship* in the hope that this will help us to see the potential structural solutions.

Why is it all so complicated?

In 2011 I wrote a book called *Finding Your Way Around Common Worship: A Simple Guide*.[1] It was designed not to reflect on *Common Worship*, but to help people to use it. The title tells you everything. It is only things that are *not* simple that need simple guides to help people to use them. The need for a book like that raises an important question about *Common Worship*. The tragedy is that *Common Worship* has become for many a byword for confusion, complication and complexity. Here is an example:

---

1 Mark Earey, *Finding Your Way Around Common Worship: A Simple Guide*, London: Church House Publishing, 2011.

[St Columba's Retreat Centre, Woking] have a sophisticated new toaster which has to be mastered if you want breakfast. Beside it is a placard with operating instructions as complicated as the preface to the *Common Worship* Lectionary.[2]

When *Common Worship* has begun to be used as a yardstick for complexity, we should hear alarm bells.

Case Study

Confusion about Daily Prayer

The other day I had a conversation with an ordinand who was struggling with *Common Worship* and the rules for a weekday service of Morning Prayer. She was aware of *Common Worship: Daily Prayer*, but finding it hard to work out how to discover what the Collect, psalm and readings were and how to find the right form of the service for the date she was due to be leading. I showed her how to find these things and pointed her to A Service of the Word and the requirements it sets out for what has to be included.

At the end of an hour's conversation, she said: 'It all seems so exclusive, as if you have to belong to some elite club to be able to have the secret key to unlock this stuff.'

Was she right? Is this stuff 'secret knowledge' or just professional knowledge? Are these simply the tools of the job? And if they are tools for the professional, does her experience still suggest that worship leading is not for amateurs?

How has a Church which says liturgy is so important ended up in this situation? The answer itself is complicated. Partly it is simply about the sheer amount of material and the number

---

2 John Pridmore, *The Inner City of God: The Diary of an East End Parson*, London: Canterbury Press, 2008, p. 171.

of volumes – the more rich you make the choices the more complex it starts to look. *The Alternative Service Book 1980* (ASB) may have been a big step for the Church of England, but it was still just one book, like the Prayer Book. It was certainly a thicker book, but in essence everything was in it – not just resources for Sunday worship but also funerals, marriage, baptism, confirmation and so on.

However, it was not long before this big but unitary book was being supplemented. The cry went up, not just from liturgists, but from those in ordinary churches and chaplaincy contexts for more material, and especially material which brought more variety. The model of 'one size fits all' was already beginning to feel outdated. In particular, two sorts of variety were sought – seasonal variety and variety of provision for different contexts. Almost as soon as the ASB was published there followed a series of further materials, some official, some unofficial, but all responding to the felt need for more. For example, within 15 years of the ASB the following had appeared:

- First off the mark was the booklet *Ministry to the Sick* in 1983, which reflected a recognition that the ASB did not make sufficient provision for the liturgical ministry of healing. It included forms of service for Holy Communion (or the distribution of Communion) following both Rite A and Rite B for use in homes or hospitals ('in the presence of the sick' as it rather prosaically called it), forms for prayer with laying on of hands and anointing, a Commendation at the Time of Death, and Prayers for Use with the Sick.
- *Lent, Holy Week, Easter*, which came out as a report in 1984 and was published for liturgical use in 1986, proved to be the first of a series of seasonal resource volumes.
- *Promise of His Glory* followed in 1991, providing seasonal resources for Advent to Epiphany.
- *Enriching the Christian Year* provided further resources in 1993. It filled in some of the gaps, particularly for saints' days and other festivals and also for 'topics' such

as 'Creation' and 'Justice and Peace'. Unlike the other two seasonal volumes, it was not 'commended' by the House of Bishops, but was produced by members of the Liturgical Commission and so came with an aura of officialdom about it.

- The Liturgical Commission report *Making Women Visible* came out as a General Synod report in 1988 and was later published more widely. It marked a recognition that the ASB's language, while 'contemporary', soon looked dated when it came to gender inclusivity. The report made suggestions for changes to numerous texts in the ASB.
- *Patterns for Worship* first saw the light of day in 1989 as a report from the Liturgical Commission. It proposed a new approach to Church of England liturgy (known as the 'directory' approach), which was based on a simple skeleton outline with accompanying resources. It included ideas for new Eucharistic Prayers as well as non-eucharistic worship. The core element of the report, A Service of the Word, came out as a separate booklet in 1993, providing considerable flexibility for non-eucharistic worship. It was followed in 1995 by *Patterns for Worship*, a fuller volume (without the eucharistic material of the original report), which included resources to use with the skeleton structure, sample services to show how to use the flexibility, and 'coaching material' to use in the training of worship leaders in the local church.
- The Franciscan-based daily office book, *Celebrating Common Prayer*, came out in 1992. Its success among clergy and others in local churches was a sign that the Shorter Form of Morning and Evening Prayer in the ASB was not proving sufficiently nourishing for many people. They sought (and in *Celebrating Common Prayer*, they found) richer and more varied forms of daily worship, which included Night Prayer and which connected with the seasons of the Christian year. Although this was not an official Church of England resource, it received approval through the Foreword written by the then Archbishop of

Canterbury, George Carey, and the lessons learned from its success were a major influence on *Common Worship: Daily Prayer* when it emerged (in its final form) in 2005.

If you pile all these books up on top of a copy of the ASB, the result is surprising: you have a pile of resources almost as tall as a pile of all the volumes of *Common Worship*. What this rather unscientific experiment does is tell us that variety, and the complexity which it brings, did not begin with *Common Worship* – it was already there. The significant difference is that before *Common Worship* it grew gradually and organically, and some of it was official and some of it was not, and (perhaps above all) it did not all carry the same name. *Common Worship* did not invent complexity and variety, but it gave it a common cover, a common name and a common logo, and it is this which makes *Common Worship feel* so much more complicated than what went before it.

The truth is that a Church which was getting used to this level of variety was not easily going to be able to put the genie back into a one-volume bottle. None of this makes *Common Worship* any less complicated off course, but it does remind us that the variety is something the wider Church in different ways had asked for, not something which someone at 'the centre' has forced upon us.

The unpredictable 'next thing'

One of the interesting points the post-ASB material reveals is that you often cannot predict what the next need will be. So, for instance, if it had been possible in the late 1970s to see just how much gender-inclusive language would move up the agenda in the early 1980s, the ASB would never have been published with confessions which included reference to our sins against 'our fellow men'.

Similarly, when large parts of *Common Worship* were being put together at the end of the 1990s, the report *Mission-shaped*

Church[3] had not been written, and few could have predicted just what a big shift there would be towards encouraging fresh expressions of church and all the implications that would have for worship in the Church of England.

At the time of the ASB, and again when *Common Worship* appeared, there were those (not least in General Synod) who expressed the hope that this change might be the last, or that this would be the final form of modern liturgy, which we could then just get on and use, and which would see us through for decades, or even centuries, as the Prayer Book had.

But this was not to be, because the nature of the beast has changed. Once any alternatives had been accepted to one simple Prayer Book, the Church of England's liturgy was to become subject to the same laws and pressures for change and evolution as any other aspects of public worship.

Repertoires of hymns and songs change and shift, slowly, gradually, but definitely. Fashions in church furnishings, vestments, styles of artwork and so on also move and change with wider cultural changes as well as from new directions in theological thinking or liturgical scholarship. Why should we think that liturgical texts should be immune to these moves? The Church of England's liturgy has only been immune to those shifts, because we chose to make it so for several centuries, allowing its printed form to become fixed and its doctrinal implications to determine its place in the legal structures of the Church. But such fixity is not by nature part of what it means to be a church which takes liturgy seriously – it is simply the particular way that developed in the particular context of the English Reformation and what followed. The result was not that Anglican worship became fixed – a cursory study of English church history since the sixteenth century makes that clear – but that *one*

---

3 Church of England, *Mission-shaped Church: Church Planting and Fresh Expressions of Church in a Changing Context* (GS1523), London: Church House Publishing, 2004.

aspect of it (the liturgical text) became fixed, while everything around it shifted and changed from place to place, from generation to generation and from one tradition to another.

However, once change is allowed, change is hard to stop. And knowing that this repeated and necessary boundary pushing will come pushes me to the conclusion that we need a new system to handle this, a system not geared towards making that change as slow and difficult as possible.

The local–national tension

A second reason for the perceived complexity of *Common Worship* is the careful balancing act going on in the Church of England between a desire to make more decisions at local level (parish or chaplaincy) and a simultaneous desire to retain some sense of national commonality. In particular, it is because of the *way* the Church of England tries to handle that tension. The way that balancing act is maintained at present is through controlling some aspects of worship by central rules and leaving other aspects to local decision.

Lectionary and the open- and closed-season approach

It is the desire to keep this balance that leads to the open and closed seasons in lectionary provision.[4] In the 'closed season', Church of England churches are required to use the *Common Worship* lectionary provision as a sign of belonging to a wider Church in which we all share the same passages of scripture. In the 'open season' local churches are invited to devise their own patterns of Scripture reading or to use lectionary modules such as those found in *New Patterns for Worship* Section C. This is a prime example of that desire to

---

4 For more on this, see Earey, *Finding*, p. 34; and *New Patterns for Worship*, pp. 103–4.

recognize the value of local decisions for local contexts, but to place it in tension with the value of feeling connected to the wider Church beyond the particular parish or church.

'Local versus centralized' or 'local versus connected'?

The tension between local and national decision-making some-times feels, at local level, like a tension between the needs of our local church and 'The Church of England', as if this latter is some sort of controlling centre. We might think of it as the Liturgical Commission, or the General Synod or the House of Bishops – some group of 'them' who feel a long way from us, who probably do not understand us, and who are trying to control us.

It may be more helpful to understand this tension as being between the local church and other churches – both local and distant, and both now and in the past and in the future. In other words, it is not primarily about keeping the centre happy, but about the centre providing a structure and framework of rules which force local churches to take account of each other. So, in the example of the open and closed lectionary seasons, the reason for restricting our ability to make local choices about readings is not so that someone at 'the centre' can control us, but so that Christians in different churches (including ours) can have a sense of being connected to other Christians by reading the same Scriptures on the same day.

Connectedness and Fresh Expressions

One of the challenges for those who are practitioners within the Fresh Expressions movement is how to make worship truly indigenous and yet connected to the wider Christian Church. Without that connection it risks becoming self-indul-gent and being disconnected from any sense of what 'Chris-tian' is – for how can we know what Christian worship looks like in a new context if we have no idea what Christian wor-ship looks like in any other context?

Hence, though the patterns and ideas from the past or from other contexts may not be the right forms for worship in this new context, they can act as a mirror and an external critique to whatever emerges from the new context.

A Methodist approach to seasonal variety

The Queen's Foundation, where I teach, has students from both the Church of England and the Methodist Church (and from some other Churches too). Here there is a particularly stark contrast between the Church of England's way of dealing with diversity in worship and the way the Methodist Church in Britain handles it.

In the *Methodist Worship Book* (MWB),[5] if you want an Advent communion service you simply turn to that service – the choices have been made for you, there is one form of service ready to use. Such an approach has much to commend it, and my Anglican students and colleagues often express the wish that CW worked in a similar way. It would certainly be simpler than wrestling with *Common Worship: Times and Seasons* and the main volume and having to print a special order of service. But there is a crucial difference – Methodists do not *have* to use what they find in MWB. Now, the truth is that Anglicans do not necessarily *have* to use what they find by way of seasonal material in CW, but the difference goes further because Methodists do not have to use *anything* that is in MWB, whereas there are certain parts of CW which Anglicans *do* have to use, and that makes the whole of CW feel very different.

You can see the difference between the Methodist approach to seasonal resources and the Anglican approach when the Church of England *does* take that 'let's keep it simple' approach. So, for instance, in *Common Worship: Times and Seasons*, there is a service entitled '*The* Liturgy of Good Friday' (my emphasis).

---

5 Methodist Church, *Methodist Worship Book*, Peterborough: Methodist Publishing House, 1999.

Does this make Anglican clergy breathe a sigh of relief that at last there is one simple service that they can follow? No. It provokes reactions like this:

- 'How can I be expected to use this service? It just doesn't fit where our church is.'
- 'Who are they to tell me what "the" liturgy is, as if there's only one proper way of doing it?'

You can see why it is hard to win in the Church of England – too much variety and people complain that things are too complex, too little variety and people feel that they are being squashed into a mould that does not fit them or their context. Anglicans are just not used to seeing services in a book as simply 'worked examples' of what might be used – they tend to see them as something that should be used as printed.

Case Study

The de-skilling of worship leaders

Though for some the Anglican reliance on a service book feels like a restrictive boundary, for others the legal framework surrounding liturgy in the Church of England produces an over-zealous desire to 'get it right' and a dependency on the rules, so that when the rules are not clear they seem to lose the confidence to make sensible decisions for themselves.

This sometimes emerges when there is a glitch with the lectionary. Sometimes people spot a genuine error, other times there is an odd coincidence of dates and holy days that means that the same reading crops up three times in a week, or something similar. One regular example is what happens about the provision for the Baptism of Christ when the Epiphany (6 January) falls on a Sunday. There are rules to determine what happens, but it gets very complicated, and often results in confused or frustrated letters to the *Church Times*.

What happens? Some people seem to go into a mild panic, because they do not know what the 'right' readings for the day are. The reliance on a lectionary that covers all eventualities and tells you what to read on what day seems to de-skill some, such that they lose their confidence in their own ability to make sensible and even Spirit-led decisions which will work for their particular context.

The point about the tension between national and local decision-making is what raises the most intractable problem for the Church of England – we now have a very broad diversity not just of practice, but of opinion about how much diversity of practice there should be, and about the levels at which certain decisions about practice should be taken.

Rules and resources are spread across many places

A further problem with *Common Worship* is the basic challenge of finding out just where the rules are. As there are so many volumes, the rules that might apply to a particular issue or question may be spread out across more than one volume, or across several different parts of the same volume.

So, for instance, a question about using the *Gloria in excelsis* during Lent might need you to check the text of the Order One or Order Two communion service, and the notes relating to all the Holy Communion services (which come at the end of the services themselves). It would also be worth checking the section of the calendar in the main volume and the general rules to order the services. And the uninitiated might also legitimately think it would be worth checking the *Times and Seasons* (or *Festivals*) volume.

Where are all the Collects?

Finding and using the CW Collect prayers is a good example of the complexity of knowing where to find material. As well as the ones printed in the *Common Worship* main volume (where they appear in both Contemporary and Traditional language versions – which makes it important to check that the ribbon is in the right section), there are now the Additional Collects (intended to be shorter, simpler and in a 'worthy contemporary idiom'), which came out in 2004, and which are published separately. They can be found on the Church of England website – but you need to know that they exist, and where to look for them – and you will not find any of that information in the main *Common Worship* volumes, because these Additional Collects came out after they were published.

The complexity of knowing where to find material is only likely to increase as parts of the CW library of resources are amended or supplemented. So far, that has been restricted to supplementary material:

- The Additional Collects mentioned above.
- The Additional Eucharistic Prayers (designed for use when large numbers of children are present), published in autumn 2012.
- The alternative texts for parts of the initiation services which, at the time of writing, are being drafted by the Liturgical Commission.

The situation will get much more complicated if and when General Synod wishes to replace material which is in the published CW volumes, rather than add to it.

A mismatch between rules and reality

Sometimes, however, the problem is a different one. The rules are fairly clear; the problem is that those rules just do not seem to match reality in any way that makes it possible to apply them sensibly.

The 'Principal Service' problem

An important feature of the way the *Common Worship* rules governing services work is the importance of determining which is the principal service. Under the rules governing A Service of the Word, this determines, for instance, whether there needs to be a confession or a Creed or an Affirmation of Faith in the service. Even in a single parish benefice with one worship centre this is not always a straightforward decision.

If the main morning service is the principal service, does that mean that those who come only to evening services need never experience confession and absolution, and need never say one of the historic creeds? This rule which seems to offer flexibility also seems to be based on a pattern where many worshippers come to church more than once on a Sunday, and therefore their diet of worship can be assumed to take in the principal service as well as a 'second' or 'third' service. The whole principal service idea itself is flawed in most churches, where people do not even come to one service every week. But for those who come only to, say, the evening service, that is *their* principal service, even if it may look like a 'second service' in the overall pattern of services in the parish or benefice.

If you add into that mix the complexities of multi-parish benefices and multiple worship centres within a parish (let alone fresh expressions of church), with the complex patterns of who gets what sort of service where and when, then the whole 'principal service' basis for decision-making starts to look much less helpful and much more out of touch with reality.

A similar issue applies to the rules about the use of the *Common Worship* Lectionary. Here, again, the relevant material is spread around generously, including in the following places:

- The Notes to A Service of the Word.
- The Notes to the Order One and Order Two forms of Holy Communion.
- The Rules for Regulating Authorized Forms of Service (main volume, p. 525).
- The Rules governing the use of the lectionary itself (main volume, pp. 539ff.).

All of this material is brought together and helpfully sum-marized in *New Patterns for Worship*, on pp. 103–4. There you will find a clear diagram which spells out the 'open' and 'closed' seasons for the lectionary, showing when the *Common Worship* Principal Service Lectionary should be followed and when local churches can choose to determine their own pat-terns of readings.

If you find those pages in *New Patterns*, this is all admirably clear. The deeper problem, in this case, is how to apply the rules in practice, because the open and closed seasons clearly differentiate between eucharistic and non-eucharistic services, with the former having much longer 'closed seasons', when the official lectionary must be used, and the latter having lon-ger 'open seasons', when local decisions can determine Bible readings.

This gets very difficult to apply if your church, like many churches, has a monthly pattern of services which includes both eucharistic and non-eucharistic services. In situations like this it is quite difficult to work out which of the closed seasons applies, and if you tried to apply the rules rigidly, then the result could be bizarre.

At this point, the more scrupulous are forced to settle for following the spirit of the law, and the less scrupulous are tempted to give up. Only the foolish would disrupt the pattern of Scripture readings over the month in order to try to follow the letter of the law. In cases like this, it is not just a question of '*Should* I obey the rules?' – it is hard to work out *how* to obey the rules.

The impact of the synodical process

The case above, of the rules governing the open and closed lectionary seasons, is an example of how the General Synod process of producing authorized liturgy can add extra complications or restrictions, which were not part of the original plan. In this case, the Liturgical Commission had been persuaded to keep the open season longer for eucharistic services as well as non-eucharistic ones, and it was the process of Revision Committees, General Synod debates, and the House of Bishops which resulted in it being kept more controlled ('an obvious flight into a fantasy world,' as Michael Vasey boldly described it).[6]

The same dynamic was at work in the production of the CW baptism service, where parts of the service originally intended as optional became compulsory by the time the services had emerged from the synodical process. The process was partly reversed by the later changes in Synod which altered some of the rubrics to make more things optional again. It is not insignificant that, in both cases, these were early parts of CW, which were authorized without having been used in experimental parishes, as the later parts of CW were.

Michael Vasey's reflections on the synodical process, as a member of the Liturgical Commission at the time, are worth hearing again:

Where [the Liturgical Commission] triggers a Protestant shibboleth, creative work may be de-railed. Where we fail to do so, sensible Anglicanism may squeeze an authentic and catholic engagement with both the Christian tradition and the world into a familiar and cosy mould. The liturgical equivalent of suburban chintz may triumph.[7]

---

6 Michael Vasey, 'A Little Cloud', in Colin Buchanan (ed.), *Michael Vasey: Liturgist and Friend*, Cambridge: Grove Books, 1999, p. 32.

7 Vasey, 'Cloud', p. 33.

Flexibility is not always made obvious

A further reason why *Common Worship* comes across as not only complicated but inflexible is because it is not easy to find the permissions for flexibility that do exist because they are often hidden in the rubrics or the notes. This is a particular problem with the Holy Communion services. One of the most common questions I have heard clergy asking over the last decade is what the simplest form of Holy Communion is. This may be because they are attempting to plan some eucharistic all-age services, or working in a fresh expression, or wanting to bring Holy Communion into their successful Messy Church service on a Saturday afternoon.

The basic answer is that the Order One form of Holy Communion is pretty flexible, and the very simplest form of Holy Communion is A Service of the Word with Holy Communion – an outline structure with a minimum of required texts.[8]

However, although Order One *is* flexible, you need to know where to look in order to find that flexibility. Knowing where to look is tricky because of a key decision made when *Common Worship* was being put together. That decision was to put the notes (which explain some of the flexibility and choices) *after* each service rather than before each service (as had been the case in ASB). The result has been that many clergy and Readers do not seem to have ever found them.

Why are the notes printed at the end of the services?

For a congregational book, there is a lot of sense in printing the notes at the end of the services, where they are less conspicuous. One of the criticisms made of the ASB was that when you turned to a service in the book, you were confronted with pages of notes before the service itself began. It

---

8 For more on this question, see Earey, *Finding*, p. 53.

made the whole thing seem complex and bureaucratic, and the aim with CW was that users of the book would find that the liturgy took centre stage, with the notes and rules discreetly placed at the end.

However, the main *Common Worship* volume, which includes the services of Holy Communion, has ended up being used much less as a congregational book than was expected, and certainly much less than the ASB was. Instead, congregations often experience the material via locally produced orders of service, or, increasingly, through words projected onto screens. This is particularly the case for services during the key seasons of the year, when the 'ordinary' version printed in the main volume is not so useful. It was always expected that congregations should use *Common Worship* in this way, as witnessed by the fact that the Church's official publisher, the same one that was publishing the CW volumes, also published a practical guide to producing local service booklets.[9] What was not foreseen was just how many churches would move to this approach and how quickly.

All of this means that even the main CW volume is often used as a leader's resource book rather than a congregational text, and in that context it is a disaster putting the notes at the end, where they can be easily missed. It is partly for this reason that when the Additional Eucharistic Prayers were published in 2012, the guidance notes were put at the beginning, with the texts following.

Let's turn, instead, to A Service of the Word with Holy Communion, which is a very flexible outline order. Here, the opposite approach is taken. Rather than print a full version of a service and then give permissions about what can be omitted, the outline is presented as the core, with notes and instructions about

---

9 Mark Earey, *Producing Your Own Orders of Service*, London: Church House Publishing, 2000.

what must be included. Finding it, though, is an issue, because it is not printed with the other services of Holy Communion, but nearer the beginning of the main volume, with the other forms of A Service of the Word. It can also be found in *New Patterns for Worship*.

Having found A Service of the Word with Holy Communion, it becomes apparent that there might be another problem. This is because the notes stress that this is not 'normally' to be used as the regular service on a Sunday – and lots of churches are only asking the question about the simplest form of Holy Communion because they *do* want to use it normally, or at least regularly, on a Sunday, for instance for an all-age communion service. *Common Worship* giveth, and *Common Worship* taketh away . . .

Funeral services – a clearer approach

It is interesting to contrast the approach taken with the Holy Communion services with that taken with the funeral provision in *Common Worship: Pastoral Services*. In that book, the Outline Order for a Funeral is printed first, with clear indications of which sections are essential and which texts must be taken from authorized provision (chiefly the Commendation and Committal prayers).

This outline service is then followed by versions of the funeral service printed in full. This gives a much clearer sense of what flexibility there is, and suggests that the simple version is primary, with various options for 'filling it out', rather than a particular form of service being primary, with some possibilities for 'thinning it down'.

The eucharistic material in *Common Worship* might have benefitted from a similar approach: printing A Service of the Word with Holy Communion (perhaps renamed as 'An Outline Order for Holy Communion') at the beginning of the orders of Holy Communion, followed by Order One and Order Two forms as 'worked-out examples'. Once again we

---

see the impact of the decision to print the forms in the main volume as if it were primarily a congregational text – the difference with the Pastoral Services volume is that it was never expected to be used in that way, but primarily as a leader's resource.

So, what happens when people cannot discover the flexibility which is built into CW? My experience is that, on the whole, they either assume that it does not exist and stick rigidly to what they find printed in the books, or that they conclude that CW is completely out of touch with their own situation, and so make their own decisions about what can be changed. Some feel bad about doing this – others do not. This brings us to a further fundamental problem.

A basic complication in the system

Whenever someone is ordained or licensed to a new parish, or admitted or licensed as a Reader, they make the Declaration of Assent, in which they make this promise:

> in public prayer and administration of the sacraments, I will use only the forms of service which are authorized or allowed by Canon.

There are two key words here: 'authorized' and 'allowed'. They matter hugely because many people assume that for the Church of England there is simply 'official liturgy' (which you pretty much have to use, and cannot really change) and 'unofficial liturgy' (which you probably should not be using, or should feel guilty about using). In fact things are more flexible – this is the good news. However, the bad news is that this means things are also more complex.

At the heart of all the provision of alternative services since the 1960s is a basic distinction between those things which are authorized and those things which are allowed.[10] In short, *authorized* means a service, or an element of a service, which is an alternative to something in *The Book of Common Prayer* (BCP).

The category of things which are *allowed*, however, is much broader. Something which is 'allowed' – as long as (according to Canon B5) it is 'reverent and seemly' and 'not contrary to Church of England doctrine in any essential matter' – could be:

- a whole service which is *not* provided for in BCP (such as a non-eucharistic Good Friday service);
- anything where a rubric says 'these or other suitable words'.

The big shift in recent years has been the invention of a type of service known as 'Commended Services'. These are basically services which fall into the 'allowed' category, but which have been produced centrally rather than locally (that is, by the Church of England Liturgical Commission), may have been discussed at General Synod (though not authorized by it) and are 'commended' by the House of Bishops as being services which are not only allowed but are considered definitely to be 'reverent and seemly' and 'not contrary to Church of England doctrine in any essential matter'. This provision has permitted the production of a range of seasonal services (for instance) over recent decades, including much of the material in *Common Worship: Times and Seasons,* in *New Patterns for Worship*, and in many other parts of *Common Worship*.

---

10 For more information on the difference between 'authorized' and 'allowed', see, for instance: Peter Moger, *Crafting Common Worship: A Practical, Creative Guide to What's Possible*, London: Church House Publishing, 2009, pp. 13–16; Earey, *Finding*, pp. 14–16; and Ian Tarrant, *Worship and Freedom in the Church of England: Exploring the Boundaries*, Grove Worship Series 210, Cambridge: Grove Books, 2012, pp. 9f.

The problem with all of this is that for the average priest, deacon, Reader, or other worship leader in a local church or a chaplaincy context, it is not transparently obvious which bits of CW are authorized and which bits are commended. All the CW volumes do include a page or two which gives this information (for example, p. 311 in *Common Worship: Christian Initiation*), but it is not easy to find, or to interpret once you have found it.

Case Study

'I've found a great [. . .]. Can I use it?'

This is a common question, and the gap in it could be filled in variety of ways:

- 'confession from some Wild Goose material'
- 'Eucharistic Prayer from the Anglican Church in Kenya' (or Scotland, or . . .)
- 'set of intercessions that I found in a book'.

This is where the rubber hits the road in terms of practicalities, because the answer requires you to have a fairly sophisticated understanding of the nuances of what is authorized and what is allowed.

This difference between authorized and allowed material also affects other things, such as whether or not you can alter the words of services and resources in CW. On the whole, if the material is in the allowed category, you have a lot of scope – so changes to forms of intercession in CW would be fine. If, however, it is in the authorized category you need to take more care, though it might still be possible because Canon B5 allows a minister to make variations which are 'of no substantial importance', even to authorized texts. The problem is, who decides whether a change is 'substantially important' or not? The answer to this is not clear.

This leaves us with a problem. I find a lot of worship leaders, having had all of this explained to them, looking bewildered and asking, 'How am I expected to remember all this?' The only honest answer has to be, 'You can't', and this in itself makes people feel nervous, de-skilled and disempowered.[11] Clergy and licensed lay ministers are being asked to promise only to use authorized or allowed forms, and yet they are not confident that they will know what those forms are. This makes them nervous both of failure and of hypocrisy.

Has *Common Worship* not worked then?

Given the challenges which we have identified with CW, it is tempting to ask whether it has failed. However, to answer that question we first have to know what it was meant to do in the first place. This is not straightforward, because *Common Worship* did not come to a 'blank sheet of paper' situation with its own aims. Rather, it was a revision of a whole raft of alternative services which had grown up over several decades. Those services were coming to the end of their authorization period, and it was that which set the agenda and the timetable for *Common Worship*.

Open-ended authorization from now on

The shift in CW to services which now have open-ended authorization ('until further resolution of the Synod') has changed this for the future. We are getting closer to a situation where the primary reason for revision of liturgical texts can be because something is not working any more, or something new is needed to supplement it, or to provide a further alternative – we can have liturgical revision with a clear purpose.

---

11 For a 'rule of thumb' which is easier to remember, see Earey, *Finding*, pp. 16f.

As a revision of *The Alternative Service Book 1980* provision, *Common Worship* has succeeded tremendously. The change-over from the one to the other went relatively smoothly for such a big shift, and churches have, on the whole, settled down to using the new resources (though not without questions and issues, as we have seen). It is when you put *Common Worship* alongside fresh expressions of church that it begins to look less successful. As a tool for that new situation it looks rather weak. It looks (to those who are trying to do the pioneering) very traditional, based on parish frameworks, traditional assumptions, and maintenance rather than missional models. In these contexts it is not working (you only need to read the blogs on the Fresh Expressions website to find testimony to that) – but then, it was not designed for this new situation.

Case Study

An ill-fitting suit?

The sense that CW needs to be stretched a very long way in order to fit is felt not only in fresh expressions of the more radical kind. Here's what one parish priest said:

> We have a church plant in a school on a new housing development. It is broadly an attempt to do straightforward, recognizable, ordinary church in a new context, but CW doesn't fit brilliantly there. Thus far we've stuck close to *Common Worship* rules, but with lots of kids, young families, a situation where it's not really feasible yet to run Sunday School separately, a need to be eucharistic, and yet a mixture of well-versed Anglicans and people who have no experience of church, it feels like an ill-fitting suit.

What does all this tell us?

There is something very striking about the pattern and nature of the questions that get asked about CW. Though there are some people who want to know what to do about the *Gloria in excelsis* in Advent, or whether you can give candles to *all* candidates at a confirmation service (or only those who were baptized), there are far more people with questions like some of those we have seen above, which are along these lines: 'What's the simplest . . .?', 'What can I leave out . . .?', 'Can I use my own . . .?', 'Is there a shorter one . . .?' and so on.

Why should that be? Perhaps it reveals a rebellious spirit or a lack of imagination? There certainly are some rebellious spirits in the Church of England, and they come from all traditions: 'The great bishop Hensley Henson once observed that a rubric saying that something shall be done seemed to a certain type of Anglican cleric a provocative challenge to his authority.'[12]

However, the real rebels are not asking the questions I have outlined – they are simply getting on and doing what they want. The people who are asking the questions are not the rebels, they are the conscientious leaders of worship who want to be true to their Anglican heritage but also want to be able to think creatively for new contexts.

These questions show that things are moving fast, and CW, despite its flexibility and variety, is still working on an older model, a model based on central control, a model now creaking at the edges. People ask the sorts of questions I have mentioned because they are planning fresh expressions, or café church, or all-age Eucharists, and they are conscious of working with the unchurched. In other words, their motives are good and often missional, but they are finding the tools the Church of England gives them are not 'bad' per se, but they are not easy to use and do not feel fit for purpose for many contexts. The context has changed dramatically, and not just from one cultural norm to another. As Steven Croft reminds us,

---

12 Stephen Sykes, 'Ritual and the Sacrament of the Word', in David Brown and Ann Loades (eds), *Christ: The Sacramental Word*, London: SPCK, 1996, p. 158.

it is no longer enough to imagine that the Christian church can change in one particular direction (such as introducing guitars or informality into its worship) and so move with the times. That may appeal to some, but it will alienate others. Different parts of our culture are actually moving in different directions.[13]

Case Study

Trying to use authorized texts in a fresh expression

Here is a perspective from one pioneering minister, working to build a new congregation in a small market town that is socially and economically polarized:

the Church of England is very dependent upon its liturgy and use of authorized texts for worship, believing that these shape us into God's people as we say the words together. However, we find many of these are words we cannot say as a community, as they do not reflect our experience of life, or of God. These are not our words; culturally they have not come out of our hearts, our streets or our struggles, and so cannot easily come out of our mouths. What happens in this situation is that many fresh expressions or new forms of church do not use the authorized texts and forms of worship, but creatively frame their own liturgy, empowering people who use indigenous language and expression to find their own authentic voice in lament and worship.[14]

---

13 Steven Croft, 'Fresh Expressions in a Mixed Economy Church: A Perspective', in Steven Croft (ed.), *Mission-Shaped Questions: Defining Issues for Today's Church*, London: Church House Publishing, 2008, p. 1.

14 Kim Hartshorne, writing on the Fresh Expressions blog, www. freshexpressions.org.uk/views/liturgy-voice#comment-3107.

It is the complexity of culture which makes it so hard to know how the Church of England can respond liturgically, for the Church of England's assumptions about liturgy were formed in a different context, in which not only was English culture more stable and less complex, but it was being moved, by political powers, in a deliberately more uniform direction, rather than a more diverse one. We shall return later to the question of how we might re-imagine a new approach which is genuinely true to the Church of England, but which recognizes a completely different cultural context and completely different assumptions about what is good and bad about that context.

For now, we conclude this chapter by focusing on a key question raised by the sheer perceived complexity of *Common Worship*: how can a Church survive which says its liturgy is vitally important to its very sense of identity, yet has key liturgical resources which are proving to be baffling, difficult and restrictive, and – as we shall begin to see in the next chapter – increasingly ignored?

2

Some Possible Solutions

A short-term solution – make the rules clearer

One thing that comes over very clearly from the previous chapter is that one of the main problems with CW is that even if the answers to the questions can be found and the flexibility does exist, it is very complicated to find the relevant information, because it may be scattered in a variety of places.

One possible solution, then, might be to try to find a way of presenting the material so that the flexibility and permissions are obvious, not hidden in rules and notes and rubrics. A halfway house is to point people to where the answers may be found and to bring some of the commonly asked questions together in one place, and in part this is what I tried to do in *Finding Your Way Around Common Worship*. However, this can only be a temporary solution, because if the services change (as they have already done and will keep doing) then the answers to the questions can change, and if the context changes (which it will) then the questions themselves change as well. The problem is more fundamental and it needs a more fundamental solution.

There is a more thoroughgoing approach, which would be to take the CW material and re-present all of it in a more consistent and simple way. At the very least, there is scope for presenting material more clearly – for instance, by putting the notes up front rather than hidden at the end, and as we have already seen, this approach has been taken with the recently published Additional Eucharistic Prayers.

The next step would be to consider ways to bring together the structure pages, the notes, the rubrics and any introductory material.

A worked example: A Service of the Word

Even something as seemingly straightforward as A Service of the Word contains a lot of detailed instructions and permissions which are distributed between: the service outline itself, which gives the bare minimum; the 'narrative' introduction to the Service of the Word section, which includes hints and tips and coaching notes as well as a few clarifications; and the detailed notes which follow the outline. So, for instance, the outline says that the Collect prayer should be included in the Preparation section or with the Prayers, but you need to read the Introduction to discover that 'The Collect does not have to be that of the day; it may be a thematic one based on the readings (in which case it should come immediately before the readings), or be used to sum up the Prayers.'[1]

Below is a table in which the material from one section of A Service of the Word (The Liturgy of the Word) is brought together. You can see the way that important information is spread between the three locations.

The service outline	The notes	The introduction
Readings (or a reading) from Holy Scripture	Normally two readings, but one is sufficient 'if occasion demands'. The reading/s could be dramatized, sung or read responsively. Readings should be taken from the lectionary during the 'closed season'.	The items in this section can come in any order, and more than once (e.g. the sermon can be split, and there could be more than one psalm). Hymns or songs can be interspersed as desired.

---

1 Church of England, *Common Worship: Services and Prayers for the Church of England*, London: Church House Publishing, 2000, p. 22.

A psalm, or, if occasion demands, a scriptural song	This can include metrical versions, responsive forms or paraphrases. A psalm may 'occasionally' be replaced by another song taken directly from scripture.	
A sermon	This can include the use of drama, interviews, audio-visuals, as well as a more traditional sermon. The sermon might be split into sections throughout the service. The sermon may come after one of the readings (not necessarily after the final reading), or later (before or after the prayers). If it is not a Sunday or Principal Holy Day, the sermon can be omitted.	The word 'sermon' is intended to be interpreted in as wide and creative a way as appropriate.
An authorized Creed, or, if occasion demands, an authorized Affirmation of Faith		On most occasions it will be appropriate for this section to have a Creed or Affirmation of Faith as its climax.

This is just one section, of one of the simplest parts of CW, A Service of the Word. It begins to become apparent just how potentially complex it would be to apply the same approach to, for instance, Holy Communion Order One. If it could be done well, it could make a big difference to those who were trying to use Order One creatively, but it would be a considerable task in itself.

The curious case of A Service of the Word with Holy Communion

A Service of the Word with a Celebration of Holy Communion is the simplest form of Holy Communion service in CW, consisting of an outline rather than a fully worked-out service. What is curious about it is that it feels very different in style from the outline order of the non-eucharistic form of A Service of the Word. 'The people and the priest: greet each other in the Lord's name; confess their sins and are assured of God's forgiveness . . .' (ASW with Holy Communion) feels less like a clear skeleton and more like an aspirational description of what a 'good' Eucharist might look like. It is not easily turned into an actual service – you have to do a lot more work with the accompanying notes in this service and in the Order One and Order Two communion services in order to make that happen.

A much clearer approach was taken in the original report form of *Patterns for Worship*, which included A Form of Service for the Holy Communion, Rite C (which was designed to go alongside Rites A and B in the ASB).[2] In the published form of *Patterns for Worship*, this became a series of instructions for combining Holy Communion with Morning or Evening Prayer or A Service of the Word.[3] If Rite C had made its way into CW as Order Three, printed with Orders One and Two in the Holy Communion section of the main CW volume, then it might have helped considerably.

---

2 Church of England, *Patterns for Worship*, London: Church House Publishing, 1989, pp. 18–20.

3 Church of England, *Patterns for Worship*, London: Church House Publishing, 1995, pp. 19, 27–9.

In practice it is hard to imagine how to present the current material in simpler ways without the result still being pretty complicated to use. It would certainly need the CW books to be re-imagined. Already most of the volumes are leaders' books rather than congregational texts, but this would need a further change, so that they were envisaged more clearly as working documents to help worship leaders put a service together, rather than texts from which the liturgy could be led – in effect the books would become printed equivalents of the *Visual Liturgy Live* software.[4]

Perhaps here we have the most realistic solution – a software-based approach to CW, rather than a book-based approach supported by software. The handling of simple presentation supported by complicated 'backroom workings' is much easier with a software- or internet-focused approach. The 'front page' of any service could then become the structure page of the existing CW services, with each element within the structure clickable, leading you to clear guidance about what is or is not permissible. This would be to take much more seriously the move from book-focused to 'virtual' liturgy. Locally produced printed editions and locally chosen projected forms of service would not be variants on the officially published books, they would become the *only* ways that forms of service would be found in print. This would be a massive shift for a 'church of the book', whose self-understanding has been focused on its prayer book.

Part of the reason that this feels such a big shift is that the idea of 'the book' has been seen since the Reformation as one of the ways of distributing power over liturgy within the Church. One of the effects of a simple one-volume prayer book, in English, used regularly and unvaryingly, was that lay people would have access to the book, and would know it themselves. The Church's doctrines as well as its liturgies for marriage, funerals, Holy Communion and so on – all were there for examination

---

4 For more information about *Visual Liturgy Live*, go to the website www.visualliturgylive.net.

and ownership by the laity, even if their production and dissemination was in the hands of a very few. In short, lay people could check up on their parish priest and would be aware of any 'dodgy' stuff, because they had a clear and available criterion and a benchmark against which their local services could be compared.

In reality, of course, this has already changed. The ASB was the last time the Church of England tried to keep its liturgy to one volume, and even then, as we have already seen, this was quickly to prove impossible. With CW we already have a situation where, even if there are CW main volumes in the pews, there are vast amounts of liturgical material which congregations are not aware of and rarely see (such as the funeral and marriage material, material for the reconciliation of a penitent, ordination services, healing services, etc.) because these are found in volumes which are not intended as congregational books and are therefore found only in the vicar's study or the parish office – if there.

And yet . . . And yet, this material, in another sense, is more accessible than ever to many people, because it is all available free of charge and well signposted on the Church of England website. It may not be under the nose of worshippers whenever they come to church, but via smartphones and personal computers it can be accessed at any time and place. The shift described above to a web-based approach would simply be the next stage of that move which has already begun.

Doesn't *Visual Liturgy Live* already provide this?

Visual Liturgy Live is the latest version of the *Visual Liturgy* software which has been around since before CW arrived. It not only provides the text of all the CW material, but also helps with the process of putting a service together. Because it is designed for ease of use, its default way of working is to present the material as you need it, taking you through the process step by step. This means that if the date and default options are chosen it presents you with full services (with all the 'propers' for the date you have chosen and with some choices for some texts), rather than generic outline frameworks. It is possible to find those basic structures and to find the notes and to display all the rubrics, but the (entirely good) desire to make it easier to use means that many people have not discovered them – in just the same way that they have not discovered them in the CW books.

All this means that for most users, *Visual Liturgy* does not currently act naturally as a reference resource which tells you what the rules are. It works well for situations where you just want to be helped to find the propers for a particular date, but not so well for helping you to see what the underlying principles or key rules might be. More fundamentally, it is currently seen as an optional extra, adding value and available for a charge, rather than as the primary way of engaging with Church of England liturgical material and rules. It is a tool for service planning, rather than the main repository of the Church of England's liturgy. For it to make that change would require considerable financial investment.

A longer-term solution – expand the boundaries

An alternative to making the rules clearer or presenting them in more friendly ways is to *change* the rules – to make the boundaries larger so that fewer things come near the boundary. Effectively this is what the Church of England has been doing for a long time now. *The Book of Common Prayer* has been changed and amended several times since Archbishop Cranmer produced an English Prayer Book in 1549. Though the changes in those early decades were fairly substantial, after the 1662 version was produced, the changes became more minor until the nineteenth century.

The 1872 Shortened Services Act (as it was commonly known) allowed for the shortening of Morning and Evening Prayer on weekdays and for making an extra service (i.e. in addition to Morning and Evening Prayer), drawing only on the BCP and the Bible with the addition of hymns and anthems. It is worth noting that even at that stage, some were worried. The liturgical scholar John Whickham Legg described it as having led to a state of 'liturgical anarchy'. Who knows what he would make of CW?[5] Then, in 1892, the law was changed again to allow extra material to be added to a 'third service' as long as it was 'substantially in agreement' with the BCP and Bible.

All of this was happening in the context of the so-called 'ritual controversy' (or 'ritual crisis', depending on your perspective). Some Anglo-Catholics were breaking the Church of England's liturgical rules (especially surrounding Holy Communion) and going to prison for what they considered to be vital pastoral and liturgical reasons. Though some argued for changes to the Prayer Book communion service, the rule-breaking was focused on the ritual aspects rather than the texts – things such as having candles on the holy table, the use of eucharistic vestments (stole, chasuble, etc.) for the priest, incense, ringing of bells at the consecration of the bread and wine, making the sign of the cross, using wafers for communion rather than ordinary bread, and so on.

All of this led ultimately, at the beginning of the twentieth century, to the Royal Commission on Ecclesiastical Discipline. It concluded, among other things, that rather than applying the law more rigorously, the law itself needed to change: 'The law of public worship in the Church of England is too narrow for the religious life of the present generation.'[6]

---

5 For more on the history of this period, see Donald Gray, *The 1927–28 Prayer Book Crisis (1)*, Alcuin/GROW Joint Liturgical Study 60, Norwich: Canterbury Press, 2005. The information on Legg is on pp. 13–14.

6 *Report of the Royal Commission on Ecclesiastical Discipline*, Chapter XI, Conclusion, quoted in Gray, *1927–28*, p. 29.

The proposed solution was to make the law of public worship broader. Letters of Business were issued to Convocations (by the crown) to set in motion liturgical revision. Liturgical civil disobedience had brought about liturgical change. The Archbishop of Canterbury, Randall Davidson, said in a speech to the Convocations:

> Rules clear in principle and yet elastic in detail we do absolutely require, if the Church, in its manifold activities, is to be abreast of modern needs and yet loyal to ancient order.[7]

The irony is that a hundred years on and despite huge amounts of revision, we still do not have these – what we have are rules complex and obscure in principle, and overwhelmed with detail: though this may not be anybody's intention, it certainly is how they are experienced by many.

Be that as it may, the law was broadened, and as the twentieth century progressed, the rules got expanded to bring *most* of the rebels within the bounds of the law. Eventually, by a slow process of evolution, assisted by the movement of clergy around the Church of England, practices which had been seen as extreme got taken on in more central parishes by non-extremist clergy, and became central and 'normal' (things such as vestments, candles, etc.).

However, what was most significant was not the changes themselves, but the new system which made further change, including alternative liturgical texts, easier. This came about, ironically, because of the failure of Parliament to approve the particular revisions proposed in the 1920s. The longer-term result was that control of liturgical matters shifted from the state to the Church, starting with the 1965 Prayer Book (Alternative and Other Services) Measure, and culminating in the

---

7 Quoted in Gray, 1927–28, p. 31.

1974 Church of England (Worship and Doctrine) Measure.[8] This process opened the way for Series 1, 2 and 3, the *Alternative Service Book 1980* and, ultimately, CW. But even this extension of the boundaries was not to prove enough. As well as the desire for more variety (already mentioned above), there was a deeper sense that a more radical shift was needed.

The 1985 report *Faith in the City*[9] was by no means predominantly about worship, but it did make some liturgical connections. It included this telling conclusion:

> to give people a 1300 page *Alternative Service Book* is a symptom of the gulf between the Church and ordinary people in the UPAs.

Is this the late-twentieth-century equivalent to the 1906 Royal Commission report? It certainly did have an impact. The report's recommendations included one, that 'the Liturgical Commission pays close attention to the needs of Churches in the UPAs [Urban Priority Areas]'.

One result of this was *Patterns for Worship*, originally a report by the Liturgical Commission to General Synod in 1989. It expressed the hope that 'The flexibility of the *Patterns* approach should help us to do what the *Faith in the City* report suggests, in . . . providing for liturgy to "emerge out of and reflect local cultures".'[10] The Liturgical Commission responded energetically to the urging of *Faith in the City*. Not only did it give time and attention in meetings to imagining what the needs of the inner cities might be, but some members of the Commission went and looked and listened, sharing worship

---

8 For more detail about the legal processes which emerged from this period, see Derek Pattinson, 'The Processes of Revision and Authorization', in Michael Perham (ed.), *Towards Liturgy 2000: Preparing for the Revision of the Alternative Service Book*, London: SPCK/Alcuin Club, 1989, pp. 85–99.

9 Church of England, *Faith in the City*, London: Church House Publishing, 1985.

10 *Patterns*, p. 2.

in inner-city contexts and talking to worshippers and church leaders there before setting pen to paper in drafting *Patterns for Worship*.[11]

The *Patterns* approach, and particularly A Service of the Word, which was a core part of the report, did get accepted and has become a central element of CW. It certainly did loosen things up, and allowed for more flexibility – but only for some parts of the service. It is significant that we are still waiting for that permission for liturgy to 'emerge out of and reflect local cultures'. At present, it can do so as long as you don't want to include a Eucharistic Prayer or a form of confession which emerges out of local culture. This is a big part of the frustration felt by many working in fresh expressions of church.

Why are we still waiting? It is because a thoroughgoing *Patterns* approach (with a focus on shape, not text) was too radical for some. The House of Bishops at the time was:

> mindful of those who want a period of stability in the liturgical life of the Church, and who might be anxious lest the Commission's proposals extend the bounds of choice and variety of liturgical provision more widely than has been customary in the Church of England.[12]

There is that word, 'bounds' – and the stress on what has been customary. Indeed, the boundary was still being seen as just that, and the bishops were thinking in terms of bringing newer forms of service (such as 'family services') within that boundary:

> The House [of Bishops] has particularly noted those aspects of the commission's proposals which could, by widening the scope of that which is allowed within statutory services, be a

---

11 See Trevor Lloyd, 'Inner City England', in David R. Holeton (ed.), *Liturgical Inculturation in the Anglican Communion*, Alcuin/GROW Joint Liturgical Study 15, Nottingham: Grove Books, 1990, p. 41.

12 *Patterns*, 1989, pp. vi–vii.

reining-in of the unco-ordinated, unauthorized and unstructured provisions which are now widespread in the context of non-statutory services.[13]

Politically, one can see the appeal of the idea of bringing new expressions within the boundary, and the whole idea has strong parallels with the way that what was seen as 'extreme' ritual was normalized by stretching the bounds.

The radical ASB quickly felt very 'yesterday'

The startling thing, looking back now on documents from the 1980s, is just how radical the ASB was seen to be – it looked 'forward to a new era of flexibility in the [*sic*] Church of England worship'.[14] It certainly did mark a significant step forward, but by 2000 the ASB was seen as much closer to the BCP, and CW was to be the 'new approach'. This is not so much a reflection on the ASB itself, but rather a sign of just how fast other things were changing in Church and society in the years following the ASB's publication.

In many ways CW does represent a new departure which goes beyond the choices and selective flexibility of the ASB. What is particularly significant about CW is the way it picks up the *Patterns for Worship* directory approach, as exemplified in A Service of the Word. This set a new pattern for Church of England liturgy which was about structures, not fully worked-out services. The idea of the importance of structure and shape is everywhere apparent in CW (note that every service in the CW library begins with a structure page). But the more radical step of providing mainly outlines rather than fully worked-out services is not so evident.

---

13 *Patterns*, 1989, p. vii.
14 *Patterns*, 1989, p. 1.

Where outlines do occur they are generally seen as extras to the main services. Note, for instance, the dilemmas when producing *Common Worship: Times and Seasons* – the titles of the services give the game away: '*The* Liturgy of Good Friday', '*The* Liturgy of Easter Day', '*The* Liturgy of Ascension Day', and so on. These are fully worked-out services, suggesting that these are the 'right' way to do them. There are some outline orders of service provided alongside the main liturgies (notably for Easter Day), but they are minor in the context of the bulk of the book. The default has been to give not just forms of service, but quite detailed forms. And whatever the intention, these are read by those for whom this is not natural territory as the Church telling them how to do everything, and then they give up, or revert to doing something more familiar, rather than engaging with the shape of the liturgy, the key elements that tradition has handed to us, and then wrestling with how to make that tradition live in their own particular context.

Flexible liturgy that feels controlling

The *Patterns* approach really was a potential game-changer, but it was not applied in a thoroughgoing or systematic way. Even where it has introduced genuine and far-reaching flexibility it can still *feel* very bounded and controlled. Why is that?

It is partly because the more bounded parts of services are the very areas where the mission questions are pressing (for instance, the need for eucharistic material in fresh expressions of church).

Fresh expressions of church and the sacraments

Those in pioneering ministry and setting up fresh expressions of church are caught between a rock and a hard place. The whole point of the fresh expressions ethos is that what is being set up are not stepping stones to 'real' church, but new expressions of what church is. The wider Church, therefore, makes clear that 'A mission initiative that does not have an authorized practice of baptism and the celebration of the Eucharist is not yet a "church" as Anglicans understand it.'[15] The problem is that the Church of England makes no provision for baptism and the Eucharist other than that in *Common Worship* or the Prayer Book, designed primarily for established expressions of church.

The other reason that the *Patterns* approach found in *Common Worship* does not always feel flexible is because where there *is* freedom it is immediately hedged about with boundaries:

- You can use A Service of the Word with Holy Communion . . . , *but* it must not 'normally' be the 'regular' service on a Sunday or weekday (CW main volume, p. 25).
- You have a huge range of authorized confessions, but the note introducing them (CW main volume, p. 122) is grudging: Prayer Book ones are fine on any occasion; 'These, or one of the forms in the services in *Common Worship* should normally be used. It may sometimes be useful to vary the form . . . , in which case one of the confessions and absolutions which follow should be used.'
- You can use Kyrie confessions, but in Holy Communion, 'This form of confession should not be the norm on Sundays' (CW main volume, p. 331, note 10).

The Synod giveth and the Synod taketh away . . .

And lastly, it is because the inherited 'mood' in the Church of England is still that liturgy is about control. When that is the case, you can expand the boundary as much as you like, but as

---

15 Church of England, *Mission-shaped Church: Church Planting and Fresh Expressions of Church in a Changing Context* (GS1523), London: Church House Publishing, 2004, p. 101.

long as there *is* one, it just feels like a very spacious prison. And that is why people still want to push at the boundaries, as we have discovered since CW.

Pushing the boundaries . . . still

A small proportion of **Anglo-Catholics** are still pushing at the boundaries, using the Roman Missal, or incorporating elements of it into Anglican services. At the other end of the church tradition spectrum are more **conservative evangelicals**, who are likely to have doctrinal concerns over things which have historically separated evangelicals from catholics in the Church of England: how sacrifice is articulated and represented in Eucharistic Prayers, how the dead are prayed about and for, and so on. They might make changes to liturgical texts to reflect their views. But these two well-established groups have been joined by a whole range of others, who are pushing at the boundaries for very different reasons:

Figure 1: Groups pushing at the boundaries.

- There are those whom I think of as the **Creatives**. For them CW is too restrictive because they want to use Eucharistic Prayers, confessions, etc. from around world, from a book they have on their shelves, or from something they found on the internet. They want the language to be more creative, or the range of images to be broader, or the symbols to be richer. They may find these alternatives in resources from the Iona Community, or the Wild Goose Resource Group, but they may equally come from the Anglican Church in Kenya, or from something 'celtic' that they found in a David Adam book, or an Australian website, whose language and imagery is more evocative, or just more eccentric. Essentially, these are people whose issues with CW are to do with creativity, aesthetics, richness and so on. CW seems to them to be dull and bureaucratic – they feel that it sounds like the product of a committee and they are looking for something that sounds more passionate and personal, that connects with heart and emotions as well as head.
- Then there are the **Radical/Progressive** types. For them CW is too patriarchal in its assumptions, too monochrome in its culture. Their concerns might be from post-colonial, feminist, womanist, queer or other perspectives. They might want to use more expansive language for naming and addressing God, to steer clear of male pronouns for the Divine, to avoid an overemphasis on purely sacrificial metaphors for the cross, and so on. Though they share some concerns with the Creatives, their main issues with CW are likely to be theological as well as (or instead of) aesthetic.
- From a very different direction come the '**New Wine-style**' churches. This naturally includes those who are formally part of the New Wine network of churches, but I am also thinking of others from a charismatic evangelical position, whether they would self-define in terms of New

Wine or not. Their worship patterns and assumptions will be strongly shaped by 'renewal' perspectives and probably by John Wimber and the Vineyard movement. Healing and individual prayer ministry are likely to be an important part of worship, as is singing in tongues and the sharing of prophetic words or images. In these contexts 'liturgy' of any traditional sort is likely to be thin to non-existent – perhaps the Lord's Prayer if you are lucky and maybe a confession if the service includes Holy Communion (though you would not necessarily get a Eucharistic Prayer – a reading of 1 Corinthians 11 might be as likely if time is short). For these churches it is not just about the words of worship, but also a whole range of associated things like robes, titles (the vicar might well be the 'lead pastor'), etc. These churches are barely able to keep to A Service of the Word, let alone anything fuller. Their main issues are to do with freedom to follow the Spirit and a sense that liturgical worship (including CW) is associated with formality and dryness, rather than a personal response to Jesus.

• Then there are those who are trying to think about worship within **Fresh Expressions** of church of various sorts – café church, Goth services, Messy Church, new monasticism, emerging church, alt.worship, and so on. For these folk the issues are likely to be about context and culture, a concern to connect with the unchurched, and a sense that CW does not do this easily or well, particularly when you try to think about incorporating Holy Communion or baptizing new members.

And in mentioning these particular boundary-pushing groups, we have not even begun to take account of the many ordinary middle-of-the-road parishes and worship leaders who bump up against particular parts of the boundary unexpectedly in the ordinary run of parish ministry.

Non-book cultures and assumptions about literacy

One of the big challenges to a church like the Church of England, which has invested so much importance in its written liturgies, is that many of those who are coming new to faith come from 'non-book' cultures. For such people, even to be given a simple printed order of service may feel culturally alien. The task is to find forms of words which may be learned by heart, committed to memory and shared. Must those words be ones which have been formed in a very different context by those who are comfortable with books, and complicated books at that? And what if this situation is compounded by the challenges of low literacy levels, or the problems experienced by those with dyslexia and other specific learning difficulties. For these people, even if books, as such, do not make them uncomfortable, asking them to navigate around complicated printed resources, or even to read quickly and easily from a screen, may be a step too far. This is not an argument for abandoning any form of liturgy, but it should make us pause before thinking that forms of worship produced for a whole national Church will automatically connect with them. It also reminds us of the value and importance of sacrament and symbol, action and movement – the other languages of worship which tend to be overlooked when the emphasis is on the texts of the liturgy.

Nothing new under the sun

Though all of these groups are raising issues which are contemporary, in another sense none of this is new. In the early seventeenth century, in the responses to the visitation questions of Bishop Lancelot Andrewes, we see evidence of puritans within the Church of England refusing to wear the surplice, treating the holy table 'as a sideboard', slimming down the liturgy in order to make more time for preaching, and not even owning a copy of the Prayer Book.[16] By the time of the Savoy conference in 1661, the puritans still wanted more local discretion over texts. Some of this sounds extremely modern.

In the early nineteenth century Thomas Arnold, in his *Principles of Church Reform* (1833), advocated the Prayer Book being used alongside 'free prayer'.[17] By the time of the 1906 report of the Royal Commission on Ecclesiastical Discipline, the commissioners were summing up the history of deviance from the letter of the law in liturgical matters in this way:

> As a matter of history, deviations from the standard set up by the Acts of Uniformity can be shown not only to have existed but also to have been tolerated in every period since the Act of Uniformity of 1559 . . . Thus, from the sixteenth century down to the present time there has existed a contrast between the theory of the law clearly expressed in the Acts of Uniformity and the practice of the clergy in the conduct of public worship.[18]

Is this a new ritual crisis?

There are some parallels in all this boundary-pushing with the so-called ritual crisis of the late nineteenth century, but there is one big difference – no one is going to prison this time. There are several reasons for that.

First, we are in a different cultural context in terms of the Church itself. We are now less likely to see matters of worship

---

16 Paul Welsby, *Lancelot Andrewes, 1555–1626*, London: SPCK, 1958, pp. 115f.

17 See Gray, 1927–28, p. 5.

18 Royal Commission on Ecclesiastical Discipline, *Report of the Royal Commission on Ecclesiastical Discipline*, Chapter III, 'Departures from the Standards of the Acts of Uniformity'.

and religion as matters over which to go to court and which can be solved by recourse to law. This is partly a result of the further separation of the Church of England from the state, so that church matters are not seen as matters for the courts and for Parliament as they were in previous generations. That change is itself related to the ritual controversies of the nineteenth century, but it means that we are unlikely to try to solve new problems in the same way.

Second, if there is one thing that the original ritual controversies taught the Church of England, it was that sending priests to prison does not stop people breaking the law where matters of principle are at stake. Prison made martyrs of the ritualist priests who were sent there, and ultimately helped the Church to see that this was no way to address the problems of public worship.

But there is also a significant element of church politics at play here. Some churches within the Church of England use the Roman Missal instead of *Common Worship*. Some churches within the Church of England use no form of externally structured liturgy at all, relying mainly on a diet of worship songs. Often (though not always) these churches, at different ends of the spectrum of church traditions within the Church of England, are large churches, with big congregations – or, at least, they are relatively well-off churches, which make big contributions to Parish Share and therefore to diocesan finances. Which bishop is going to make too much fuss about their liturgy (or lack of it) and risk losing not only their goodwill, but also their cash? And realistically, how would one go about prosecuting them? Who would accuse them, and what would be the penalties that could be applied if they were found wanting? In reality, the pastoral fallout in a Church which relies on goodwill would be unsustainable, not to mention the bad press and bad feeling in the congregations themselves and the wider community.

The fact is that we are in a different place. Bishops prefer to see themselves as partners in ministry, not as regulators of worship. However, the Church of England does still structure its worship through canon law and liturgical text, note and rubric, and I want to suggest that once again we are at a 'Royal Commission' moment. I am not suggesting that we need another Royal Commission. What was crucial in the end about the Royal Commission which reported in 1906 was that though it was set up to enquire into ecclesiastical discipline, it ended up concluding that 'the law of public worship . . . is too narrow . . .'. What began as an enquiry into discipline ended up pointing the way to a need for new rules.

Any of the groups listed above as boundary-pushers might seek to make the changes that they look for in one of two ways:

- they might simply get on and do it, without regard for the structures and Canons of the Church of England or (for those who are authorized ministers) for the vows they took at ordination or at their admission as Readers; or
- they might try to seek some sort of special permission or dispensation to stretch or cross the boundaries, or to make the particular changes they want.

This second approach – seeking special permission – brings us to another strategy which could be applied more generally.

A different strategy – let bishops give local permission

Making the existing rules clearer, or expanding the boundaries by making the existing rules broader are both strategies which we have, to some degree, already tried. An alternative approach is to allow for the rules to be stretched in focused or limited ways for specific contexts. Bishops already have some discretion about liturgical matters in their own dioceses, given to them by the Canons.

The bishop's power to make local exceptions to general rules

An example of the sort of discretion given to bishops is found in Canon B14A. This allows a bishop to dispense with the normal canonical requirement for Morning and Evening Prayer to be said and Holy Communion to be celebrated in every parish church on every Sunday and principal Feast Day. The permission, however, only applies to the church for which it is sought and can only be given for good reason, after taking into account the services offered in other churches in the area. Permission must be sought by the incumbent and Parochial Church Council acting jointly.

Some among the groups of boundary-pushers I have outlined are more likely to ask for permission than others. Now that the Church of England has affirmed the importance of fresh expressions of church alongside the parish system, it *feels* as if that permission is more likely, and the expectation that the Church has made provision for experimental liturgy and a freer approach in these contexts is high. People therefore often turn to their bishop to ask for guidance or even permission. Some bishops even give this 'permission', writing letters of support, sometimes with guidance about where they draw the line, or with the requirement that authorized worship must be available at other times or elsewhere in the parish.

The expectation that this permission can be sought or given is, however, misplaced. If something is allowed, you can do it without permission: and if it is not allowed, not even a bishop can give you that permission, unless the Canons specifically provide a power of dispensation in that particular case for the bishop to exercise.

Case Study

All-age Eucharist at St Philip's

Paula had been in post as Vicar of St Philip's Church for six months and was turning her mind to how to 'attract more families and children to church' – something that the advert for her post had said the PCC were enthusiastic about.

She met with a small sub-group of the PCC and they decided to suggest a bold new pattern of worship which extended their provision of all-age worship. There was already a non-eucharistic all-age service on the first Sunday in the month, but they were keen to make the Eucharists on the other Sundays of the month all-age as well. The non-eucharistic all-age service was very informal and had been growing over the previous few years, so Paula was keen to make sure that the eucharistic services were not a huge jump for those who had become worshippers at the monthly all-age service, but had never really come to any other services.

She remembered some creative liturgies, which also seemed child-friendly, which she had encountered when she trained for ordination, and she reached for them now on her shelves. She found one that seemed to fit the informality she was looking for, and which would not need very much adapting to the particular circumstances at St Philip's. There was just one problem – she was aware that the liturgy she wanted to use was not part of *Common Worship*, and she knew there were a lot of rules about what you can and can't use in the Church of England. She decided to write to her bishop.

The bishop was delighted to get her letter. This was just the sort of creative, outward-focused approach to worship that he was trying to encourage in the diocese. The problem was, Paula wanted to use material that wasn't authorized, and for a service of Holy Communion that was a particular challenge. The bishop was stuck – he wanted to encourage Paula, but he also felt trapped by the rules about Holy Communion. In the end he wrote back, encouraging her to proceed, but asking her to use one of the authorized Eucharistic Prayers from *Common Worship*, or one of the Additional Eucharistic Prayers recently authorized, even though they are not supposed to be used weekly for Sunday worship. He also had to ask her to change the wonderful confession in her planned service and try to turn it into a Kyrie confession so that it fell within the *Common Worship* rules, and to make sure she always included one of the Creeds or authorized Affirmations of Faiths. He didn't dare mention that A Service of the Word with Holy Communion, on which the new services were based, was not meant to be used regularly as a main Sunday service. As he signed the letter he almost wished she hadn't asked him, but had just got on with it. As Paula read his letter, she felt the same.

One possible solution to the current situation, then, might be to give to bishops that wide power of dispensation which sometimes they think they have and sometimes other people expect them to have. This is not a new idea. In the 1906 report of the Royal Commission on Ecclesiastical Discipline, the commissioners noted that many bishops seemed to think that they already had the right to give permission or exemptions from the letter of the law at their own discretion, a right that they felt was an ancient one passed on from the earliest days of the English Church.

A claim has been advanced that a power resides in each Diocesan Bishop to control the public services of the churches in his diocese, and to authorize additions and omissions therein to an extent which no witness has exactly defined, but which is apparently supposed to cover a larger area of immunity from the requirements of the Acts of Uniformity than any construction of the shortened Services Act would warrant. This right, under the name of *jus liturgicum*, was claimed definitely by at least two Bishops, and less distinctly by another, as a power inherent in the Episcopal office, which has never been specifically taken away from Bishops of the Church of England.[19]

They continue:

There cannot, in our opinion, be any doubt that the Acts of Uniformity bind Bishops as well as other clergymen [*sic*]; and that the law does not recognize any right in a Bishop to override the provisions as to services, rites, and ceremonies contained in those Acts. The question whether the law ought not to be modified so as to confer on the Bishops wider powers of authorization, and also control, of public services, than any they at present possess, is an important one to which we shall return at a later stage of our Report. At the present stage it is enough to say that, though Bishops have from time to time used a certain liberty of action with a view to relax the stringency of the Acts of Uniformity, it does not appear to us that there is any legal ground for assuming that, apart from statutory provision, the Bishop of a diocese has an inherent right to dispense the clergy from observing the provisions of those Acts.

A similar appeal to this supposed ancient right of bishops to regulate worship, this *jus liturgicum*, was made in the wake of the defeat in Parliament of the proposed 1928 Prayer Book. The House of Bishops proceeded on the basis that the use of the defeated book would not be considered by individual bishops as 'inconsistent with loyalty to the principles of the Church

---

19 Royal Commission, *Report*, Chapter III, 'Departures from the Standard of the Acts of Uniformity'.

of England'. Again, the lawfulness of the bishops behaving in this way has been challenged.[20]

As we have noted, many bishops today give explicit or tacit 'permission' to forms of service or patterns of worship which are not technically allowed under canon law or the rules of *Common Worship* or the Prayer Book, but which seem to the bishops to be appropriate mission-focused responses to particular contexts or the needs of particular groups of people. I suspect that for most bishops these days this is not because they have a strong sense of this permission-giving being an ancient right, but because they increasingly recognize their role as not only chief pastor in the diocese, but chief missioner and evangelist. Where parish clergy are suggesting patterns which seem responsible, well thought through and pastorally and evangelistically sensible, bishops want to be seen as people who say 'Yes' rather than those who are always resisting change or fresh ideas. Few bishops today want to be seen as the anchor holding back the mission-shaped ship.

Adapted ecclesiological structures, but not liturgical ones

What is interesting is that a permission to work in this way in relation to liturgical needs has not been part of the thinking that has come out of the *Mission-shaped Church* report. That report has led to subsequent adaptation of the structures of the Church, particularly as it impacts on the parochial system, with the establishment of Bishops' Mission Orders. Central to this 'principled and careful loosening of structures' (as Archbishop Rowan Williams called it in the General Synod debates of 2004)[21] is the role of the bishop.

---

20 See Will Adam, *Legal Flexibility and the Mission of the Church: Dispensation and Economy in Ecclesiastical Law*, Farnham: Ashgate, 2011, pp. 2, 121–31.

21 Quoted in Steven Croft, 'Fresh Expressions in a Mixed Economy Church: A Perspective', in Steven Croft (ed.), *Mission-Shaped Questions: Defining Issues for Today's Church*, London: Church House Publishing, 2008, p. 6.

The principles undergirding it are, first, the possibility of there being legal flexibility for the higher purpose of the protection or promotion of mission and evangelism and, second, on the presumption that the appropriate person to permit such flexibility, by means of mechanisms akin to dispensation or economy, is the bishop.[22]

What is interesting is that there has been no suggestion of a parallel 'principled and careful loosening' or adaptation of the liturgical rules of the Church of England.

What liturgical guidance is there for fresh expressions of church?

Fresh expressions of church and pioneering situations are covered by the recent legislation in the *Dioceses, Pastoral and Mission Measure*. It was Part V of this Measure which made provision for Bishops' Mission Orders. These allow the bishop to make provision for pioneer ministry and new expressions of church alongside the inherited patterns of church in the geographical parishes in which they may take place. You might expect that this new framework would give clear and full instructions about worship in these exceptional (though increasingly common) situations, but this is not really the case.

If you explore further, you find that there is a Code of Practice which relates to Part V of the Measure. Search even further and you eventually find some fairly brief instructions about worship tucked away in Appendix 3 to the Code of Practice. When you look more closely, however, the basic gist of what is said there is this: You will need to be flexible and creative, taking account of context, but you will need to do this within the frameworks already established in the Canons and *Common Worship*.

---

22 Adam, *Legal Flexibility*, p. 89.

It is even more important to remember that this advice is not for what one might consider the 'safer' end of fresh expressions of church, such as a new service for children and families on a Saturday evening, or a Messy Church congregation. The Code of Practice envisages that, 'Normally, there will be no need for a Bishop's Mission Order where the development is wholly or largely within and by a single parish. Support and oversight is offered by the Bishop and wider church family to the new initiative through the existing diocesan and parochial structures.'[23]

No, this guidance is for the more 'extreme' examples of fresh expressions of church, expressions which cannot be 'held' within existing models, and where the needs are likely to be mostly 'outside the box'. It is these emerging church contexts which are told that all they need is provided by *Common Worship*, and that the rules which govern their liturgical life are the same as those governing all other expressions of church in the Church of England. Whatever else one might think of this guidance (which in many respects is great) it seems a little unrealistic.

Bishops' Mission Orders effectively provide to bishops (on a statutory footing) a degree of dispensation and discretion which can be applied to parish boundaries.[24] Is it possible to envisage a liturgical parallel to Bishops' Mission Orders? Should we consider the provision of 'Bishops' Liturgical Orders', which would apply to contexts of mission and properly enshrine a bishop's ability to give dispensation from the normal rules in particular circumstances for a particular purpose?

---

23 *Dioceses, Pastoral and Mission Measure*, Code of Practice to Part V, Section 1.2.5.

24 See Adam, *Legal Flexibility*, for more on the whole concept of dispensation in church law.

Local liturgical projects?

There is one situation in which there is already some provision for existing liturgical rules to be laid aside in carefully controlled ways, and that is through the Ecumenical Canons (Canons B43 and B44). Through them provision is made for some of the normal requirements for worship to be dispensed with, either under particular ecumenical circumstances or in Local Ecumenical Projects (LEPs) (which are now generally referred to as Local Ecumenical Partnerships).

These provisions include the possibility of Anglican ministers using the rites of other Churches, and ministers of other Churches presiding at Anglican rites. They include the sort of long-term and big-picture vision in planning which I am suggesting – the bishop is to use the powers given, taking account of what other Anglican services are being offered in other churches in the benefice or locality, so that decisions are made not just on the basis of what is included in this service this week, but on an overall diet of worship for a congregation and the overall provision in a geographical area. There is still a certain Anglican defensiveness in evidence, because congregations are to be informed in advance of a service of Holy Communion what form of service it will be and which minister will be presiding, and no service based on the rite of another Church is to be 'held out or taken to be' (Canon B44.4.3.b) a service according to the rites of the Church of England.[25]

Central again to these provisions is the role of the bishop (alongside incumbents and PCCs) for giving permission, especially where the permission being sought is for regular use. However, these provisions are limited to a narrow range of ecumenical situations. Perhaps this also gives us a model for how bishops could take a central role in a more broadly framed provision for some sort of 'Local Liturgical Project'.

One could argue that, because ecumenical working and missional thinking is now central to all that we should be doing as

---

25 For more on this, see Adam, *Legal Flexibility*, pp. 79–82.

a Church, such suggested provision (Bishops' Liturgical Orders and/or Local Liturgical Projects) should be extended more widely, not just for designated ecumenical areas, or designated mission projects, but for any parish which can make a good case for it.

The Eucharist – some existing thinking

It is tempting to think that the most vexed question would be how to provide guidance about what was appropriate or essential Anglican content and shape for a service of Holy Communion. In fact, considerable thinking about this has already been done in relation to the Ecumenical Canons, and especially to the situation in LEPs.

The Code of Practice which goes alongside Canons B43 and B44 addresses the question of what happens when an Anglican priest is invited to preside at Holy Communion according to the rite of another Church. The bishop's permission is to be sought, and the Code goes on to list the elements of a Eucharist which would need to be included in any service which the bishop might be asked to approve:

- The proclamation of the Word of God.
- Preparation of the bread and wine.
- Thanksgiving over the bread and wine for God's acts of salvation in Jesus Christ.
- Prayer and the words of Christ's institution of the sacrament.
- The breaking of the bread.
- Eating and drinking in communion with Christ and with each other.

The Code goes on to list additional elements, which, 'although of lesser importance, are normally desirable in some form':

- Act of repentance and declaration of forgiveness.
- Confession of faith.
- Intercession for the whole Church and for the world.
- A sign of peace and reconciliation.
- Anamnesis or memorial of the great acts of redemption.
- Invocation of the Holy Spirit on the community and the eucharistic action.

It then adds that 'the Church of England values a reading from the Gospels' and 'values the regular use of the traditional creeds'.[26]

Solutions revisited

Though the situation is in many ways very different from that which existed at the time of the ritual controversies, many of the sentiments expressed in the report of the Royal Commission could be applied in some ways to the current situation. For instance:

In an age which has witnessed an extraordinary revival of spiritual life and activity, the Church has had to work under regulations fitted for a different condition of things, without that power of self-adjustment which is inherent in the conception of a living Church . . .[27]

The regulations and assumptions which govern worship, though they have been adjusted, are still 'fitted for a different condition of things'. The Church nationally has been given a 'power of self-adjustment'. What has not happened, and needs

---

26 Church of England, *Ecumenical Relations: Canons B43 & B44 – Code of Practice* (1989 with 1997 supplements), London: General Synod, 1989, 1997, paras 78–80.

27 *Report of the Royal Commission*, Chapter XI, Conclusion.

to happen, is for that 'power of self-adjustment' to be applied at a more local level.

Michael Vasey reminds us: 'The room given in the *Alternative Service Book* for unscripted prayer and local decision marks a return to the norm for Christian prayer.'[28] The key point he is making is this: we have forgotten that Anglican assumptions about liturgy have been shaped by a social context at the time of the Reformation in England in which control of worship was part of political control. We are not in that situation any more: we need to behave differently.

In this chapter we have considered possible responses to the problems outlined in Chapter 2. First, we considered the simplest option: try to bring the rules together to make them clearer. This would certainly help, but it would be a short-term solution, and would not solve the more challenging problems raised when the rules do not seem to fit new situations.

Next, we considered the possibility of enlarging the boundaries, stretching the rules to bring more practice within them. This is a solution that has been tried repeatedly. We have been changing the rules to make the boundaries larger for a long time now, but though it has eased the pressure in the short term, in the longer term it has not worked: the result is simply that the pressure points on the boundary change and move.

But there is a deeper problem. The reason that the expanding boundaries approach needs to be abandoned is not because it cannot work but because the boundaries mindset just does not sit well alongside a flexibility mindset. The boundaries approach works on a legal model, breeds a lack of trust, and produces at local level a mindset which is based on, 'What can we get away with?' rather than 'What would be good worship for this context?'

---

28 Michael Vasey, 'Modern Ordinands and the *Book of Common Prayer*', in Margot Johnson (ed.), *Thomas Cranmer: Essays in Commemoration of the 500th Anniversary of his Birth,* Durham: Turnstone Ventures, 1990, p. 279.

Finally, we looked at ways of allowing more local (that is, diocesan) scope for exemptions from the rules for particular contexts or situations. Here we have some precedents or patterns provided by Bishops' Mission Orders and Local Ecumenical Projects, and it might be possible to make them work more broadly. However, I want to ask a more fundamental question, which is whether the legal framework model is the best one for our current context, and whether it is producing worship which is the best we can offer.

In the mid-twentieth century, there was a radical shift to move to the Church controlling its liturgy more directly. We need another radical shift – this time not just about *who* controls liturgy (the shift from a Prayer Book controlled by Parliament to alternative authorized services controlled by the Church) but about the fundamentals of *how* liturgy is controlled, and at what level. Chapter 3 will attempt to name and articulate an alternative approach, and Chapter 4 will then spell out what the implications might be of moving towards it.

3

A New Approach and a Different Solution

From a boundary to a centre

Up to this point I have been talking about *Common Worship* and about liturgical understanding and practice in the Church of England in terms of boundaries – a boundary formed initially by the content of *The Book of Common Prayer*, later expanded to include other features which were consonant with it and supplemented by forms of service which were authorized as alternatives to it. We have considered what lies within the boundary, and seen that there are those who still wish to challenge, test and expand the boundary, pushing at the limits. We have seen that one of the ways the Church has responded has been to stretch that boundary. But thinking in terms of boundaries is not the only way to categorize worship or to evaluate the appropriateness or not of particular forms of service.

Set theory

The Christian anthropologist and missionary Paul Hiebert has helped the Church to draw on the insights of mathematical set theory to explore different ways of categorizing things.[1]

---

1 Paul G. Hiebert, *Anthropological Reflections on Mission Issues*, Grand Rapids: Baker Books, 1994, pp. 110–36. A shorter summary is given in Paul G. Hiebert, *Transforming Worldviews: An Understanding of How People Change*, Grand Rapids: Baker Academic, 2008, pp. 33–6.

He points to two variables which apply when people and cultures categorize things.

Intrinsic or extrinsic?

One variable is to do with whether things are categorized *intrinsically* (that is, according to qualities or attributes which they have in and of themselves, irrespective of their relation to others) or *extrinsically* (that is, according to their relationship to other things or to a common reference point).

Well formed or fuzzy?

The second variable is to do with whether the category is well formed or 'fuzzy' – that is, how clear the boundaries are. For some sets there is a clearly defined boundary and you are either in or out. In this digital approach, there are only two possible answers and nothing in between.

For other types of set the edge is blurred – belonging is more like a continuum where you can tell if you are in, and you know clearly when you are out, but there are places in between in which it is less clear. This sort of categorization is analogical rather than digital. Hiebert uses the example of when day turns to night. Both day and night are clear in themselves, but there is a phase between the two in which it is not possible to be certain which category you are in. In a fuzzy set, membership is a matter of degree.

Four possible combinations

When you put together these two variables you get four possibilities:

- Intrinsic and well-formed sets – which he calls 'Bounded sets'.
- Intrinsic and fuzzy sets.

	Well formed	**Fuzzy**
Intrinsic	*'Bounded'*	
Extrinsic	*'Centred'*	

Figure 2: Four types of set.

- Extrinsic and well-formed sets – which he calls 'Centred sets'.
- Extrinsic and fuzzy sets.

The question is, can we use a similar approach to help us understand and define the category 'Church of England worship'?

There are important aspects of set theory which we can draw on to put alongside the bounded-set approach. In particular there are valuable insights to be drawn from the fuzzy-set approach and from the centred-set approach.

Applying set theory

Paul Hiebert applies these set-theory approaches to world-view and missiological issues and particularly to the questions, 'Who is a Christian?', 'What is a church?' and 'What constitutes mission?', giving answers from each of the four perspectives. Drawing on his work, Tim Dakin has reflected on how the different approaches might apply more generally to the Anglican Communion and how the Communion

defines who belongs and who does not – a critical issue
for some as proponents and opponents of the proposed
Anglican Covenant fight it out.[2] The Anabaptist theologian, Stuart Murray, applies Hiebert's model to questions
of ecclesiology in his *Church after Christendom*, reflecting
on how the different models apply in Christendom and post-
Christendom Churches.[3]

Bounded sets

An obvious ecclesiastical example of a bounded set is a parish –
if you live within the parish boundary, you have certain rights
(e.g. be buried in the churchyard, get married in the church, be
baptized in the church, and so on.). The chief criterion is geographical and is digital. There is only a yes or no answer – you
cannot be 'partly in the parish', though you can be very near
the edge of the boundary.

As we have seen, historically we have also used this approach
to control our worship. For centuries, acceptable and allowable
Church of England worship was what was in the BCP, which provided the boundary. Still today, though other services are authorized, they are alternatives to that book. The boundary has been
expanded, but it is still ultimately related to the Prayer Book.

Fuzzy sets

The other sort of intrinsic categorization in Hiebert's model is
the intrinsic fuzzy set. There are two crucial things about an
intrinsic fuzzy set:

- You can belong by degrees.

---

2 Tim Dakin, 'CMS and New Mission II', *Anvil*, Vol. 25, No. 4,
2008, pp. 283–303.

3 Stuart Murray, *Church after Christendom*, Milton Keynes: Paternoster Press, 2004, pp. 26–31.

- You can belong to more than one set at a time.

These may be of great value when thinking about the question of what makes Anglican worship Anglican. First, because it makes it possible to think of Anglican as something that you can be 'more' or 'less' or that you can be 'becoming', so that there are more options than simply 'Anglican' or 'not Anglican'. In the world of fresh expressions of church and alternative worship, this is a much more helpful way of understanding, because many of the criteria which are applied to evaluating worship are criteria which would apply equally to 'good' worship in other traditions. So, is it possible for worship to be Anglican and (say) Baptist at the same time? In the bounded-set approach this is not easy to picture, and even in a centred-set approach it may be problematic, but in a fuzzy-set approach it is possible. This opens the door for greater ecumenical working in liturgical terms, making it possible for a service to be both Methodist and Anglican at the same time, rather than forcing LEP congregations, for instance, to define whether the service this week is Anglican *or* Methodist according to which book or liturgical text is used, or which minister presides. The question no longer has to be 'Is it Anglican?' but can become 'Is it Anglican *enough*?' or 'In which ways is it Anglican?'

Centred sets

Turning now to centred sets, the key aspect of this approach is its relationality.

Centred sets in Anglicanism

An obvious example of a centred-set approach in Anglicanism is the place of the Archbishop of Canterbury. In one sense, the Anglican Communion has been a group of Churches with a relationship to the Archbishop of Canterbury. The Anglican Covenant process shows us that this sort of

---

approach can make people nervous and seek greater clarity about how the centre operates and what it means to be in relation to it.

The Church of England also operates what is essentially a centred approach to doctrine. Note how the Preface to the Declaration of Assent (made at ordinations, for instance) lists some core Anglican documents (including the 39 Articles and *The Book of Common Prayer*) but requires only a declaration of '*loyalty* to this inheritance' as 'inspiration and guidance'.[4] In other words, you do not have to sign up to agree with everything in them, only to a 'loyalty' to them – a very different thing. The centre is clear: the boundary more complicated and unpredictable.

Worship offered by a group of Christians might be appropriately called 'Anglican' not because of the particular content of the service, but on the basis of the relationship between that group of Christians and other Anglican churches, and between that group and an Anglican bishop. It could be the relationships and lines of responsibility, support and accountability that make it appropriately 'Anglican', rather than an adding up of how many key liturgical elements are included in each service.

In centered-set thinking, greater emphasis is placed on the center and relationships than on maintaining a boundary, because there is no need to maintain the boundary in order to maintain the set.[5]

Centred sets can also be defined in terms of 'moving towards' a particular centre, rather than moving away from it.

---

4 See Church of England, *Common Worship: Services and Prayers for the Church of England*, London: Church House Publishing, 2000, p. xi.

5 Hiebert, *Anthropological*, p. 124.

Here the overlap with a fuzzy set is clear: a church's worship can be 'moving towards' *Common Worship* or the Prayer Book (or aspects of them), and still be defined as Anglican. It is the direction of travel, rather than having arrived at the destination, which allows the category 'Anglican' to be appropriately claimed. Here, once again, is a useful approach to help those in Anglican fresh expressions of church to evaluate their worship.

> Some things are far from the center and others nearer to it, but all are moving toward it. They are, therefore, equally members of the set, even though they differ in distance from the reference point. Things near the center, but moving away from it, are not a part of the set despite a proximity to it.[6]

The question is not 'Are we using the right texts or structures?', but 'Are we heading in the right direction in relation to those texts or structures?' To put it another way, 'Are we running away from what has historically formed Anglican worship, or are we moving towards it, albeit warily, cautiously and with an eye to the needs of our particular context?' When the centre is itself flexible (as CW is) then moving towards it does not mean that worship which is properly Church of England will inevitably revert eventually to following BCP or using the CW books – it means that they will show some family likeness, and use some common material, without necessarily taking on a ready-made package. As Michael Moynagh puts it, they will have 'something of the denomination's DNA without being a clone'[7] – identity without uniformity. Put another way, the key question would be 'Is there a *relationship* with historical Anglican patterns and contemporary Anglican worshippers?'

---

6 Hiebert, *Anthropological*, p. 124.
7 Michael Moynagh, *Church for Every Context: An Introduction to Theology and Practice*, London: SCM Press, 2012, p. 366.

Water hole or boundary fence

The difference between bounded and centred approaches is sometimes illustrated by the contrast between sheep farming in Britain and sheep farming in Australia. In Britain, you need boundary fences to keep them in; in Australia, you simply dig a water hole – they'll come back!

Drawing the threads together

There are helpful insights from both the fuzzy and the extrinsic approaches, and it might be natural to put them together and expect to find the combination in the fourth way of forming a category, the extrinsic fuzzy set (which some writers, though not Hiebert, call the 'open set'). Hiebert, however, says little about this fourth category, pointing out that there has been less writing about it. He seems to struggle to apply it to mission and church, and in description it risks sounding like no kind of category at all, with no centre and no boundary, so that everyone belongs or no one does.

For our purposes, I want to put the two approaches of the centred set and the fuzzy set together in a particular way. I suggest that we consider how Church of England worship would look if we categorized it as a centred set with a fuzzy centre (or where at least some aspects of the centre could be fuzzy).

The centred aspect allows us to define Anglican worship as something to do with relationships – to whom and what do a group of worshippers relate, and how do they relate to it? It includes structural questions about which other Christians they are linked with but also questions about which traditions they relate to, look towards and draw upon. It is important to remember that in Hiebert's analysis, the centred set is a well-formed set with boundaries – 'Things related to the center naturally separate themselves from things that are not'[8] – that

---

8 Hiebert, *Anthropological*, p. 124.

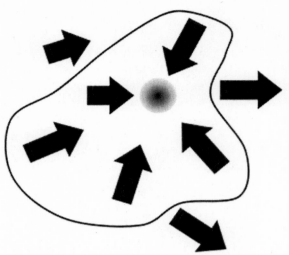

Figure 3: Centred set with a fuzzy centre.

is, it has clarity about whether you are in or out, and it is not another way of talking about a completely shapeless free-for-all.

The fuzziness at the centre allows us to recognize that there can be a degree of uncertainty or flexibility about at least some of the things which stand at the centre, and allows for the centre to be defined by qualitative elements as well as quantitative ones. This allows us to recognize that being Anglican can be about 'becoming', growing, maturing, holding to Anglican values, or developing an Anglican approach or an Anglican tradition, rather than just ticking or crossing a series of boxes which determine whether we are in or out.

In general in what follows, the most important distinction I want to draw is between the bounded-set approach and the centred-set approach, and I will use these two basic terms for convenience. But when I talk about a centred set, I am recognizing that aspects of the centre may also be fuzzy.

Short-term and long-term approaches

One of the implications of a bounded-set approach to worship is that it forces us to think in short-term ways, which reinforce legalistic approaches. It is a pattern which focuses on the detail of this particular service: Was it in accordance with the Prayer Book or *Common Worship*? Were all the required elements present? Which texts should have been authorized ones, and were they?

One of the consequences of a centred-set approach is that it would open up the possibility of, and the need for, a more long-term approach. It would still be possible and necessary to assess some aspects of an individual act of worship to see whether they were 'tending towards' the centre or not, but it would be equally important, and would become equally natural, to look at the bigger picture and to consider the longer term. Evaluation of worship would mean looking at patterns of worship as well as individual services; it would mean considering services over a period of time to ask more long-term formative questions about the overall balance, the long-term biblical coverage of the readings, the general approach to the sacraments or the theological balance of the songs. This approach would tend to develop strategic, rather than short-term, thinking, and would recognize the way that worship forms us over time, not just in each individual service. It would allow us to acknowledge the cumulative impact of worship as well as the instantaneous, and would lend itself to an evaluative and accountable mode of operating, rather than a legalistic one.

Applying set theory to recent practice

In worship terms the Church of England has operated both approaches. We have seen that the BCP has been an historic boundary, though much expanded and supplemented in recent decades.

If we turn to hymnody and song, however, the situation is very different. For songs and hymns, the Church of England has taken a centred approach – there has never been an authorized hymnbook, but there is a certain 'range' which has pointed towards the Anglican-ness of what was being done (books such as *The English Hymnal, Hymns Ancient and Modern,* or *The Anglican Hymnbook*). In more recent years, of course, that centre has changed and grown (some might say it hardly exists any more), just as the boundary of liturgical text has changed.

More recently, we have some experience of using the centred principle for liturgical text as well, through the arrival of 'commended' services alongside authorized services. For worship which is not catered for in the BCP, the Canons allow a minister to use anything which is 'reverent and seemly' and 'neither contrary to, nor indicative of any departure from, the doctrine of the Church of England in any essential matter'. Commended services are effectively services which the House of Bishops commend as fulfilling those criteria. The *centre* is being defined (Church of England doctrine and a sense of reverence and seemliness – whatever that means), but the boundary is not neat, and the bishops do not have to justify their commendation in a rigid, objective way.

Common Worship: Daily Prayer as an example of a centred approach

The *Daily Prayer* volume of CW gives us a good example of what it might mean to have some texts which act as benchmarks rather than boundaries. The rules about what must be included in a Church of England weekday service of Morning or Evening Prayer are covered by A Service of the Word. This makes the services in *Common Worship: Daily Prayer* worked examples of A Service of the Word, rather than forms which are compulsory or exclusive in their published form. Within that volume, certain parts of the service are marked as necessary and others as non-essential, but in fact this simply denotes a sort of internal consistency. The only absolutes are what are required by A Service of the Word, which for weekday worship are pretty minimal, and don't require any specific texts other than the Lord's Prayer.

Hence the Church of England has a published set of resources, which express its corporate mind on good practice in forms of daily prayer, but which act as benchmarks against which you could measure local forms, rather than boundaries which would exclude local forms.

The same principles apply not just to formally commended services, but to other aspects of services where the CW rubrics already allow some scope, such as the topics at intercessions or the allowance of 'other suitable words'. How do you know whether other words are 'suitable'? Presumably by comparison with the sort of thing which CW itself gives us. This is a relational criterion, a centred approach.

An evolving core of texts

The approach to the tension between local choice and central control which *Common Worship* assumes was helpfully worked through in a book of essays written by the Liturgical Commission, called *The Renewal of Common Prayer*.[9] One of the ideas outlined in that book is of an 'evolving core' of texts alongside a clear sense of common structure or shape to services.

What is not spelt out in the book is how that core of texts is determined, or how it is to evolve. What we have seen in the years since is the raising of further questions: 'How many

---

9 Michael Perham (ed.), *The Renewal of Common Prayer: Unity and Diversity in Church of England Worship* (GS Misc 412), London: Church House Publishing/SPCK, 1993.

people need to know some texts for them to be part of the core?' 'Can they be core if they are not used in every Anglican service every time?' 'Does it matter that we know them in a version not shared by others (for instance, the unique Church of England version of the ecumenical modern Lord's Prayer text)?' Fresh expressions of church have focused the question more sharply: 'How soon in the life of a new "church" do such core texts need to be introduced in order to preserve the Anglican nature of the church's life and worship?' Increasingly these can feel like 'deck chairs on the Titanic', questions in the face of far bigger challenges about connecting an increasingly unchurched or dechurched culture with any sort of Christian worship.

Graham Cray has suggested that some of the core might be centrally determined (e.g. key texts at baptism) whereas others might 'evolve' by 'popular assent' (e.g. the Collect for Purity). Presumably he is suggesting that these latter texts will survive simply because they are used, as liturgical market forces determine which texts become known, remembered and passed on. Such texts therefore become seen as core by sheer fact of being used often.[10]

Essentially, this is how a core repertoire of hymns and songs develops in a local church or within a denomination. It is not fixed by outside decision, though it may be shaped by decisions such as which hymns and songs get published in books, and it allows for local decision in terms of which songs and hymns actually get used and form the repertoire of a congregation. It is also not fixed for ever: musical repertoire is constantly adapting as new material is added and other material which seemed right in an earlier age is quietly dropped from use, as it no longer speaks to a new generation.

---

10 Graham Cray, 'Common Worship – Common Mission', *Faith and Worship*, 71, Trinity 2012, p. 12. This was originally an address given at the Diocese of Liverpool Liturgical Conference on 25 February 2012.

Learning from other Churches

What we need is to shift entirely and consistently to a centred-set approach for all aspects of Church of England liturgy, and take away the 'boundary' mentality altogether. This may sound radical and perhaps dangerous to some in the Church of England, but it is not without precedent in other Churches. Maybe we can learn from a Church which already works with a centred-set approach – the Methodist Church in Britain. This is a Church with whom we are in a covenant relationship, so perhaps this is one way in which the Church of England can learn from our covenant partner.

An important starting point is to recognize that worship in Methodism is not a free-for-all. There is an official resource, the *Methodist Worship Book*. This is authorized by Conference as 'a standard for Methodist worship' (MWB, p. viii). You do not have to use it every time or in every place, but it provides a benchmark against which anything else can be judged.

- The book contains a set of services which you can see as 'default' settings, starting points, examples of appropriately Methodist and Christian worship.
- It also contains some guidelines, such as the very clear guidance about how to structure a service of Holy Communion and a Eucharistic Prayer,[11] for those whose Methodist tradition includes the importance of extempore prayer.
- The Methodist system also includes the expectation of accountability through the quarterly Local Preachers' Meeting. This meeting brings together all those responsible for leading worship in a circuit – the local preachers (i.e. lay preachers), presbyters, deacons who are preachers, student presbyters and probationers. Others who contribute to worship (such as church stewards, worship leaders and musicians) may also be invited to the meeting.

---

11 Methodist Church, *Methodist Worship Book*, Peterborough: Methodist Publishing, House, 1999, pp. 221-2.

Each meeting is meant to 'consider the state of the work of God in the Circuit so far as the role of local preachers and worship are concerned', and to 'hold local preachers accountable for their ministry, considering in particular their character, their fidelity to doctrine and their fitness for the work'.[12]

There are, of course, significant differences in ecclesiology and polity between our two Churches. In particular, the circuit system (and the standard five-year tenure for ministers) has a significant impact in ironing out idiosyncratic practices of ministers and local preachers in Methodist worship.

However, the key to understanding the system as it operates in Methodism is that the system is essentially one of trust rather than one of control, and that has a huge impact on how it feels at grass roots. Methodism has learnt the lesson of liturgical history:

Basic agreement on theological interpretations, therefore, still leaves room for a variety of liturgical expressions not only in the ancient churches but in the churches today. A unity in faith does not necessitate a uniformity in eucharistic texts or eucharistic practice.[13]

This is not to claim that this system makes for perfect worship in Methodism – there are plenty of Methodists who would challenge that – but it is a different structural approach, and it engenders a different 'feel' in relation to worship in Methodism from the legalistic model of the Church of England. And there is little evidence that the Church of England model is producing worship which is of any greater quality.

---

12 See Standing Orders 589 and 560 of the Methodist Church, available at www.methodist.org.uk.

13 Paul F. Bradshaw and Maxwell E. Johnson, *The Eucharistic Liturgies: Their Evolution and Interpretation* (Alcuin Club Collections 87), London: SPCK, 2012, p. 356.

Applying this to the Church of England

If we applied the principles of a centred set to Church of England worship, what would we put at the centre? As we have already seen, the idea of a 'core' to Church of England worship, focused around shared structures and some common texts, is not new, but was the basis on which the Liturgical Commission worked on *Common Worship*. What is different about the suggestion here is the way that core would operate – not as a barrier to be policed, but as a centre to be 'tended towards'. I suggest that the centre could consist of four sorts of thing:

- The Church of England's doctrinal core – the articles, the Prayer Book (this time as a repository of doctrine), the ordinal – those things to which clergy and other licensed ministers already assert their loyalty.
- A particular book or set of services. The Prayer Book would be part of this, but could be supplemented by *Common Worship* services. These would be the benchmark liturgical texts against which others were measured and tested, but they would no longer form a boundary.
- A set of practical liturgical guidelines, which might include advice about how to structure services (the sort of thing already in *New Patterns for Worship*).
- A set of Anglican liturgical principles, which might especially help those in pioneering or fresh expressions contexts to reflect on what it means to lead a new church whose worship is intending to be 'Anglican'.

This last point about what it is that makes worship 'Anglican' raises some interesting issues in itself. It has proved notoriously difficult to define Anglican worship, though some have made an attempt. The next chapter gives us a chance to explore this important area in more depth.

4

What Makes Worship 'Anglican'?

As we have seen, a shift from a bounded-set to a centred-set approach would need us to clearly define what is at the centre, because it is the centre that would provide us with the criteria against which to assess worship in the Church of England.

Does it matter?

Any degree of agonizing over what makes Anglican worship 'Anglican' raises a further question. If we can agree that worship will shape us as Christians, and that it will particularly play a part in shaping those who are new to the Christian faith, is it not enough that worship should shape us as 'mere' Christians? Just how important is it that these new Christians are shaped as Anglican Christians? For the purposes of this book, I am assuming that for those of us who find ourselves in this part of the Church, who recognize good things in this particular tradition, and who see that worship is part of what defines Anglicans, the question about what makes Anglican worship 'Anglican' needs to be worked through. But it is also important to acknowledge that for others, and in the big scheme of the Kingdom of God, whether worship is Anglican or not is not the most significant question.

Part of the problem here is that for so many centuries, despite much variation on the ground in how worship took place, there was one key text (the BCP) and a shared sense that commonality itself was a good thing and part of what it is to be Anglican.

This began to crumble as parts of the wider Anglican Communion began to make their own decisions about liturgy, especially in the post-colonial era of the twentieth century. As Christopher Irvine puts it,

> As we map, both historically and geographically, the authorized liturgical usage around the Communion, the use of a single book emerges as a matter of ideology rather than a description of actual practice.[1]

We have already seen that in England, too, the twentieth century brought to a head some of the tensions that had been rumbling under the surface for decades.

Some thoughts about commonality

The notion of commonality has been key to Anglican assumptions about worship from the very origins of the Church of England, as the titles *Book of **Common** Prayer* and ***Common Worship*** testify. In colloquial use, something which is 'common' is something cheap, something of poor quality, something so prevalent as to be devalued. But the word 'common' also has other associations – of familiar resources and patterns, of pulling together, of shared identity, of something in which we all have a stake, of space that belongs to all (like the village common).

---

1 Christopher Irvine, 'Introduction', in Christopher Irvine (ed.), *Anglican Liturgical Identity: Papers from the Prague Meeting of the International Anglican Liturgical Consultation*, Alcuin/GROW Joint Liturgical Studies 65, Norwich: Canterbury Press, 2008, p. 5.

'Commonality' is also a concept which begs a question: 'In common with whom?' At the Reformation, commonality in worship was about asserting identity (of England over against Catholic Europe) and about control (both political and religious). Michael Vasey reminds us that, 'unity is a way in which the strong police the weak'.[2] Stuart Murray similarly reminds us of 'the influence of Christendom which standardized, and exported as normative, what began as local and contextual forms of worship'.[3] How do we ensure that a good desire to remain connected to one another does not become a means of a group or groups within the Church, who have power and influence, suppressing other voices? How might it be possible for common prayer to mean something co-operative, collaborative, experimental, something that can develop and change organically, something that allows space for difference, for mistakes and for taking risks?

Part of the deep problem for *Common Worship* is that it is trying to face in two directions at once. On the one hand it is trying to provide flexibility, openness and variety; on the other it is trying to reassure some in the Church of England that we still have some sense of common prayer and worship, not just in the sense of *The Book of Common Prayer*, but in the sense of something that is shared across the whole Church of England.

So, where would one look for some guidance about what 'Anglican' worship should look like? David Kennedy suggests three basic convictions:[4]

2 Colin Buchanan (ed.), *Michael Vasey, Liturgist and Friend*, Cambridge: Grove Books, 1999, p. 37.

3 Stuart Murray, *Church After Christendom*, Milton Keynes: Paternoster Press, 2004, p. 89.

4 David Kennedy, *Understanding Anglican Worship: A Parish Study Guide*, Grove Worship Series 130, Nottingham: Grove Books, 1994, pp. 4–9.

- Anglican worship gives a central place to Scripture.
- Anglican worship witnesses to the importance of the Holy Communion.
- Anglican worship has a special concern for the building up of the body of Christ.

Most other attempts to give some shape to the concept of Anglican worship give far longer and more complex lists. One of the most recent attempts at this is found in Michael Perham and Mary Gray-Reeves, *The Hospitality of God*, a book about fresh expressions (or 'emergent church' in the USA). This lays out 20 principles of Anglican worship:[5]

1 Liturgy is ordered with beauty and holiness.
2 Liturgy is the normal way Anglicans worship God together. (By which they seem to mean that there is some structured intentional framework to worship, typified, but not dependent on, printed service books.)
3 A degree of commonality in liturgy is needed to maintain and enhance the unity of the Church. (They go on to talk about an Anglican 'family likeness' which is not a strait-jacket, but derives from a Communion that used to look to a shared prayer book as a source of unity.)
4 The Christian formation of the people of God individually and as community takes place within the celebration of the liturgy.
5 Our doctrine is derived from our liturgy (*lex orandi, lex credendi*).
6 Scripture, both as lection and as song (psalms and canticles), is always present in our liturgy and we read it in step with one another through the use of common lectionaries.
7 There is enough repetition for some texts to 'enter the memory and feed the soul'.

---

5 Michael Perham and Mary Gray-Reeves, *The Hospitality of God*, London: SPCK, 2011. The list here is summarized from pp. 11–22.

8 Liturgy normally includes a prayer of thanksgiving, penitence and intercession, some prayers in 'collect' form, creed and blessing, and principal services include a sermon.

9 Liturgy is dialogue (i.e. there are spoken texts for the congregation, as well as hymns and songs).

10 In any liturgy, there is usually a reference to the Trinity, prayers are offered through Jesus and the Spirit is invoked.

11 There are distinctive roles in the liturgy for the orders of the Church – laity, deacons, priests and bishops.

12 The laity express their participation in liturgy both by what they do together and by what individuals are called out to do as representatives of the people.

13 Liturgy is normally led by ministers ordained or authorized by the bishop and the president of the Eucharist is always a priest or a bishop.

14 Liturgical shape is more fundamental than liturgical text.

15 Movement and gesture are not over-prescribed, but normally have a place in the liturgy.

16 Liturgy usually includes music: Anglicans value hymnody, sing Scripture as well as read it and recognize that music deepens the experience of worship.

17 Ordained ministers and others leading worship usually wear distinctive liturgical vesture.

18 Worship is connected to the seasons of the Christian year.

19 Canon law describes who may be invited to receive Holy Communion.

20 Anglicans feel free to draw selectively on the liturgical traditions of other communities.

Those principles are an interesting mix of what sound essentially descriptive (e.g. no. 16 about valuing music) and what sound more prescriptive (e.g. no. 19 about who can receive communion, or no. 8 about some expected content). These principles are not related specifically to the rules of any part of the Anglican Communion, and they describe how Anglican worship has been rather than what it should be. They also point out that it is not the case that all of the principles would be agreed by all Anglicans, or indeed be present in every Anglican church. What they are offering is a range of principles or values that cumulatively give a 'feel' for what Anglican worship looks like. On their own, none of them 'defines' Anglican worship, but if *none* are present worship would not feel distinctively or authentically Anglican at all.

Importantly, they address the assumption that emergent churches are simply rebels. They talk about churches which are in many ways on the edge, but which are, at the same time, 'working very much within the flow of Anglican liturgical principle and practice'.

> There is a widespread suspicion in the inherited church that the emergent churches within Anglicanism do not take canon law in relation to worship, or indeed the whole ethos of Anglican liturgy, seriously. We found that there were some quite important areas where the emergent churches are at variance with the rest of the church, but the overall picture was, to our mind, one where, consciously or unconsciously, emerging church leaders and congregations were working very much within the flow of Anglican liturgical principle and practice.[6]

That sense of going with the 'flow' is essentially about a centred rather than a bounded approach. It is possible to spot worship which is going against the flow, but the key is relationship and fluidity, not textual box-ticking.

Working with the centred-set approach

Perham and Gray-Reeves give a good example of what a centred-set approach might look like in practice. They describe one of the American emergent churches in which *The Book of Common Prayer 1979* of the Episcopal Church is used as a source of shape and some words, as a standard and a core, even while its every word is not followed. In this

---

6 Perham and Gray-Reeves, *Hospitality*, p. 11.

emergent church, the shape of collects is taught to the worship leaders, and then they are expected to be able to create them themselves.[7] There is a clear core which sets criteria for evaluation and gives a benchmark, but the local church leaders are trusted to relate to this centre in appropriate ways.

This does not sound that far from the way Eucharistic Prayers are described in the document known as the Apostolic Tradition of Hippolytus from the third century: if you have a competent leader, let them pray their own prayer; if not, copy this one.[8]

A similar approach to what one might call 'improvising on an Anglican theme' is described by Bishop Lindsay Urwin. In relation to the sacraments, he suggests (from an Anglo-Catholic perspective) that we have been over-focused on protecting their validity and efficacy by ensuring the use of authorized words and should instead seek to ensure 'loyalty to the doctrine of the Spirit at work in the encounter'.[9]

Reflecting on the ordination service for Derek, a youth missioner, as priest for the fresh expressions youth congregation, Eden, he writes:

> So, alongside the questions about the 'how to' at Eden, we had to ask what was essential to ordination, in order to make it clear that we were doing something that belonged to the whole Church . . . I may have played a little fast and loose with the Canons at this ordination, but have no doubt that had second- or third-century Christians been present . . . they would have known what we were doing.[10]

---

7 Perham and Gray-Reeves, *Hospitality*, p. 84.

8 See, for instance, Geoffrey Cuming, *Hippolytus: A Text for Students*, Grove Liturgical Studies 8, Bramcote: Grove Books, 1976, p. 14.

9 Lindsay Urwin, 'What is the Role of Sacramental Ministry in Fresh Expressions of Church?', in Steven Croft (ed.), *Mission-shaped Questions: Defining Issues for Today's Church*, London: Church House Publishing, 2008, p. 32.

10 Urwin, in Croft (ed.), *Mission-shaped Questions*, p. 33.

Urwin's approach is to work towards a 'lively doctrine of exceptions', which allows us to name clearly the norms, and then also to work with clear criteria for exceptions.[11] There is value in this approach, as discussed in Chapter 2, but it entrenches notions of which sorts of churches count as 'normal' (where, presumably, the norms apply without exception) and which ones might be considered exceptions. The centred-set model is more flexible and also more consistent in allowing for the answers to those questions to be kept open.

Building blocks from the Liturgical Commission

The Church of England Liturgical Commission for the quin-quennium 2006–11 also gave some thought to what mission-focused Anglican worship should look like, coming up with what it called 'Building Blocks for Mission-shaped Worship'. These are a list of 18 bullet points, and most of them are general 'good things' (e.g. worship that: works for the good of the world; is wholeheartedly sacramental; engages with both Old and New Testament; encourages participation; inspires creativity). However, most are not specifically related to being Anglican, and there are only two that seem to focus on something more concrete: 'Absorbing core Christian texts (e.g. the Lord's Prayer)' and 'Maintaining imaginative engagement with *Common Worship* values and frameworks'.[12]

---

11 Michael Moynagh, *Church for Every Context*, London: SCM Press, 2012, pp. 375f., makes a similar case for exceptions, recognizing that they can, in time, become new norms, but affirming this as natural organic development.

12 For more on this, see Ian Tarrant, *Worship and Freedom in the Church of England: Exploring the Boundaries*, Grove Worship Series 210, Cambridge: Grove Books, 2012, pp. 7f. (NB Tarrant talks about 19 bullet points, but the original document only seems to contain 18.)

Anglican liturgical style

Kenneth Stevenson and Bryan Spinks edited a volume called *The Identity of Anglican Worship* in honour of the liturgical scholar Geoffrey Cuming. In a chapter called 'Is there an "Anglican" Liturgical Style?' David Stancliffe offers some reflections:

> there is an elusive but very distinctive Anglican style, which has a lot to do with the acceptance and integration of a number of different layers, which create a sense of unity by inclusion, rather than of uniformity by exclusion.[13]

This idea of unity by inclusion rather than uniformity by exclusion is a significant insight and also adds to a broad sense of what it is to worship in an Anglican way. Once again, this is a centred-set approach. This is reinforced by Kenneth Stevenson's reflections in the concluding chapter, that 'we seem to have moved in our collective instincts to a looser view of liturgical norms, as embodying tradition rather than law'.[14] He is right that in our instincts we have moved from law (bounded set) to tradition (centred set) – but we have yet to catch up with that move in our structures.

A move towards Anglican liturgical values

Steven Croft gave a keynote presentation as part of the Liturgical Commission's National Liturgy Conference in Oxford in 2005, on fresh expressions of church and worship. In it, he also wrestled with some of these issues. He later wrote this up and took his ideas further in *The Future of the Parish*

---

13 David Stancliffe, 'Is there an "Anglican" Liturgical Style?', in Kenneth Stevenson and Bryan Spinks (eds), *The Identity of Anglican Worship*, London: Mowbray, 1991, p. 133.

14 Kenneth Stevenson, 'Anglican Identity: A Chapter of Accidents', in Stevenson and Spinks (eds), *Identity*, p. 186.

System.[15] He suggests we have moved from a unity defined by common worship texts, to unity defined by common worship shapes. He says that even this is now breaking down (particularly under pressure from fresh expressions of church), and he thinks that the next step is to define the unity of the Church of England and, by extension, perhaps of the Anglican Communion, in terms of common values which lie at the core of our corporate life and of our Anglican heritage. He proposes that these might be the Chicago–Lambeth Quadrilateral (Scripture; the historic Creeds; the sacraments of baptism and Eucharist; and episcopacy with a threefold ordering of ministry), with the addition of the Five Marks of Mission (which are, in summary: proclamation of the Kingdom; nurturing new believers; loving service; transformation of unjust structures of society; and safeguarding creation).

What all the examples I have given above seem to suggest is that Croft is right – text-based boundaries are not the way forward either for the Anglican Communion or for the narrower question of what constitutes Anglican worship. Texts still have a part to play, but as part of a set of values, used in a centred, not boundary-forming, way.

The idea of common worship shapes has been important in CW and in wider ecumenical thinking. However, when we come to Church of England specifics, the fact that the Prayer Book service of Holy Communion has such a different shape from CW Order One means that any claim for universal shapes for worship has to be fairly cautious. And so we turn to Croft's focus on values.

What are the liturgical values for Anglicanism?

The values that Croft suggests are helpful, but because they are all values which the Anglican Communion has suggested for

---

15 Steven Croft, 'Conclusion – Unity and Diversity in a Mission-shaped Church: A Suggestion', in Steven, Croft (ed.), *The Future of the Parish System: Shaping the Church of England for the 21st Century*, London: Church House Publishing, 2006, pp. 178–82.

ecumenical discussion and agreement, they are, by definition, not too distinctively Anglican.[16] Furthermore, for our purposes we might need some values which are more specifically focused on worship. Here, the seventh International Anglican Liturgical Consultation, which met in Prague in 2005, may help us. 'Anglican Liturgical Identity' was its focus, and in his introduction to some of the papers from the consultation, Christopher Irvine outlines what he calls three 'core principles' or tendencies of Anglican liturgical life, and distinguishes them from a further list of 'features' of Anglican worship.[17] His core principles are, in summary:

1 Anglican worship is structured and ordered, and there is a connection between the Church's doctrine and its worship (for more on this, see below).
2 Anglican worship is corporate, both internally (there is a part for all to play) and externally (the worshipping community must never be disconnected from the wider community and the outworking of justice in society).
3 Anglican worship gives a central place to the public, corporate reading of the Bible in structured, planned and accessible ways.

In his first principle, he emphasizes the value of shared structures, with flexibility over content. This certainly feels an accurate description, but we need to take account of Croft's suggestion that we have moved on from common structures, and we also need to recognize that a focus on structure has been a shared, and not just Anglican, emphasis in recent years.

There is, however, a deeper sense in which there is something specifically Anglican about the idea that worship should be *consciously* structured, rather than accidentally structured or structured in a hidden way. That means that it is a structure which we articulate, and which can therefore be discussed, challenged and

---

16 See Moynagh, *Church*, p. 371, where he makes the same point.
17 Irvine (ed.), *Anglican Liturgical Identity*, pp. 8–11.

owned by the wider Church. The shape of our worship is something we make ourselves accountable for, rather than being a
matter for each local congregation to decide independently. Even
this idea is not exclusively Anglican, but the way it is applied and
the balance between the local and the national does feel particular
to the Church of England, compared with other denominations
which also value structure in worship.

In his second principle we perhaps see echoes of the Anglican
Communion's origins in a national church, established by law,
and in conscious relationship with the political structures of
the country. We also see something of the Reformers' emphasis
on re-balancing the power between clergy and laity in liturgical
decision-making.

In his final principle we again see something related to the
historic origins of the Church of England as a Church of the
Reformation, with a particular emphasis on the regular reading of Scripture in public as a means of nurturing the faith of
the people, and the consequent development of non-eucharistic
worship as a key feature of its liturgical diet, alongside Holy
Communion.

Though we might want to add to these principles, or suggest alternatives, what Irvine helpfully does is to separate these
from a further list of more specific 'features':[18]

- The inclusion of corporate confession in public worship.
- The connection between our worship structures and our
  ecclesiology, and in particular an episcopal ecclesiology.
- Trinitarian baptism, and the importance of both baptism
  and Eucharist.
- An 'aesthetic sensibility' and commitment to 'quality' in
  language, music and the arts in worship.
- The importance of the Christian year and daily prayer.
- The valuing of the psalms.
- The use of a blessing of the congregation at the end of
  worship.

18 Irvine (ed.), *Anglican Liturgical Identity*, p. 10.

There are some interesting overlaps with other lists we have already considered, and also some interesting particular features (for instance, the inclusion of a blessing at the end of a service). Like the other lists, it includes both concrete items of content and rather more vague ideals or principles. Crucially, he states, 'These principles are neither prescriptive, nor intended as a check-list to exclude, but an attempt to map out some general defining qualities.'[19] He is recognizing that the job of discovering Anglican liturgical identity has to do with a cumulative approach, rather than some kind of 'sufficient' list.

Irvine goes on to recognize that in the context of the Anglican Communion, one may need to speak of plural Anglican identities rather than one single identity. This may be a helpful approach to take even in the more limited context of the Church of England, where, as we are discovering, the concept of what is Anglican, or even what *feels* Anglican, can vary from place to place and from tradition to tradition.

This becomes particularly obvious in the key discussion document which was produced by that Prague meeting of the International Anglican Liturgical Consultation (IALC).[20] This includes some further lists of Anglican features of worship and also gives four stories of Sunday worship from different parts of the Anglican Communion and different parts of Anglican tradition. What is striking about these four accounts is not the shared features as much as their sheer diversity. The lists that precede the stories are divided into three sections:

- 'Ethos/Elements' – which includes things such as the balance between word and sacrament, the holding together of catholic and reformed emphases, the provision of authorized texts but with freedom for a variety of expression, the

---

19 Irvine (ed.), *Anglican Liturgical Identity*, p. 11.

20 'Appendix: Liturgy and Anglican Identity – A Discussion Document by the International Anglican Liturgical Consultation, Prague, August 2005', in Irvine (ed.), *Anglican Liturgical Identity*, pp. 46–56.

connection between private devotion and public worship, and the importance of worship taking place in an 'ordered liturgical space'.

- 'Characteristics', such as the use of the Lord's Prayer, responses and Creeds, and the importance of intercession in public worship, baptism and Eucharist.
- 'Emphases, trends and aspirations' – which gathers together some theological areas such as the importance of incarnation and creation, and the eschatological direction of Christian worship.

They contain the same mixture of specific content items, significant features and theological emphases that we have seen in other lists, but once again it is hard to discern what is descriptive and what might be prescriptive about these lists.

Indigenous and catholic

Another key worship-focused value for the Anglican Communion might be that our worship should seek to be truly indigenous and truly catholic. Rowan Williams reminds us that this, after all, is the key thing that the first Prayer Book was aiming to be: a form of worship connected (though selectively) with what had gone before, but designed for 'this realm'. For the newly formed Church of England at the Reformation:

Its liturgy is, accordingly, designed for this place; it does not intend to be a universal form of Christian worship. To put it at its most positive, the first Anglican liturgies refuse to consider the Christian congregation in general or in abstract.[21]

---

21 See Rowan D. Williams, 'Imagining the Kingdom: Some Questions for Anglican Worship Today', in Stevenson and Spinks (eds), *Identity of Anglican Worship*, p. 6.

He goes on to point out the irony that the subsequent history of Anglican worship has been tied to the idea of the Prayer Book as a 'timeless model of worship', when it was designed to be exactly the opposite: concrete and specific, for both place and time.

The beauty of the authentically indigenous

This idea of an Anglican worship-value being the importance of something grounded and contextual connects back to something else which Michael Perham and Mary Gray-Reeves explore. They write about 'beautiful liturgy, meant to move the soul, drawing us closer to God'.[22] They are talking about an Anglican aesthetic core. But then they surprise us – this is not just 'high-brow culture' of a Radio 3 sort, but both an aesthetic beauty *and* the beauty of something authentically indigenous, which enables a group of people to be truly themselves before God and to offer that corporate self to God. The beauty of being true to yourself and your context is part of Anglican liturgical 'ethos' just as much as the beauty of choral evensong.

If there is a core value for Anglican worship here, then, it is that it should be radically contextualized, and if the Prayer Book was radical in being a 'local' book for the whole of England, the modern equivalent might be forms of worship which are 'local' in a much narrower sense, as long as they continue that other important principle, which is to be connected to (though not identical with) worship which has gone before.

Inculturation, contemporary worship and the Prayer Book

There are those for whom the notion of an inculturated liturgy for contexts in England has gone too far and given

---

22 Perham and Gray-Reeves, *Hospitality*, p. 37.

too much attention to the receiving culture (i.e. the particular place or people for whom the worship is being designed) and not enough to the inherited tradition of the Church of England – that is, as they see it, *The Book of Common Prayer*, which can be seen as somehow 'native' to the English context. John Scrivener, for instance, talks of the importance of 're-connecting those who have lost touch with resources native to their own culture' (that is, the Prayer Book), rather than 'approaching them as if they were cultural aliens'.[23]

There is clearly much truth in the idea that English culture has been shaped by the Prayer Book, but the reality is also much more complicated than this. For a younger generation in particular, the Prayer Book may not feel like a 'native resource'. Though they may come to love and appreciate the Prayer Book, it is more likely to be akin to the way that teenagers come to love and appreciate the taste of tea or coffee. It is a taste one can come to appreciate, but not necessarily one that appeals or connects at first encounter. And it must be first encounter issues which are a priority for the Church today.

This is not to say that there is no place for Prayer Book worship in the mission of the Church today. But where the Prayer Book does appeal to those on the edges of the Church, I would suggest that it is often because it gives a sense of mystery or of the 'other' (which may or may not be about divine transcendence), not because it naturally connects with the rest of their lives. It may therefore be part of mission, but mainly because it becomes itself part of the pick-and-mix culture in which we live. 'I go to Prayer Book services because I like them', not because they are simply what the Church gives me; or 'I like certain aspects of Prayer Book worship' (language, sense of history, being able to connect with worship of former generations, etc.), while

---

23 John Scrivener, 'Paradoxes of "Inculturation"', *Faith and Worship* 71 (2012), p. 6.

rejecting other aspects of the world-view from which it comes (for instance in the assumptions it makes about women's role in church or society, the place of the monarchy it exhibits, or its theology of marriage).

As we have seen, the Prayer Book is itself a form of inculturated liturgy. That inculturated form went through several different editions (1549, 1552, 1559, 1604, 1662) as the context in England (both social and theological) changed. And if the Prayer Book brought a unity to worship in England, it did not do so because it was universally liked or appreciated (the Cornish rebels were not the only ones who did not like it, being joined later by the Puritans and others) but because it was enforced. It is printing which reinforced the sense that the Prayer Book was to be enduring; it is not clear that those who produced it either in its early or revised forms expected that. And while it brought a uniformity to worship in England, it simultaneously cut English worship off from the worship of the Churches of Europe, both Catholic and Protestant (including Lutheran and Reformed traditions).

One of the ironies of the twentieth-century liturgical movement, including the way it has impacted on liturgical revision in the Church of England, is that though it may have resulted in a further splintering of worship in the Church of England, it has also brought us closer to other Churches, both Protestant and Catholic, through the emphasis on shared structures and shapes to worship (especially eucharistic worship) and some sets of words which we share in common with other English speakers around the world.

A more focused list

Patterns for Worship, starting from its 1989 report form, has also recognized the importance of discerning what lies at the heart of Anglican liturgical identity. It lists the following (an interesting mix of values and more specific content items) as 'some of the marks which should be safeguarded for those who wish to stand in any recognizable continuity with historic Anglican tradition':[24]

- Recognizable **structure**.
- Emphasis on reading **Scripture** and using **psalms**.
- 'Liturgical' words, **repeated**, some **known by heart**.
- Using a **Collect, Lord's Prayer**, some **responsive** forms.
- Centrality of the **Eucharist**.
- Concern for **form, dignity** and **economy of words**.

Compared to the longer lists we have already considered, this seems at first much more manageable and concrete. However, this list immediately highlights some of the bigger problems with defining 'Anglican worship' which we have already encountered.

First, it is much easier to do *descriptively* than it is to do *prescriptively*. The Anglican Church does not have one formative hero to whom the tradition looks back. The nearest we have to a single figure is Thomas Cranmer, primary architect of *The Book of Common Prayer*, but because he changed his views and his liturgy during his own lifetime, people afterwards have tended to pick the slice of Cranmer that most accords with their own views of what is right or good, so his example is less useful as a criterion or critique of any contemporary claim to true Anglicanism. The only way to define prescriptively an Anglican pattern of worship is to point to the Prayer Book itself. Once that is no longer deemed sufficient, it is much harder to know where to turn for principles which would be true to that book without being dependent on its texts.

The second problem follows on from the first, which is that having realized that one has to settle for a descriptive definition, that description itself is often contested. A description of Anglican worship depends heavily on what era of Anglican

---

24 *Patterns for Worship* (GS 898), London: Church House Publishing, 1989, p. 5. The bulleted list is my paraphrase.

history one looks to and, in more recent centuries, where in the world one looks, and even within England, which part of the Church of England spectrum of traditions one looks at.

The inclusion of 'centrality of the Eucharist' in the list above is an example of this. This was certainly part of Cranmer's vision, but not part of the practice which he was able to bring about, because in the aftermath of the Reformation many were reticent to receive communion, not having been used to doing so thus far in their lives. 'Centrality of the Eucharist' would be a good description of much of the Church of England in the latter part of the twentieth century, following on from the influence of the Anglo-Catholic revival of the late nineteenth century, but it would not apply to most evangelical parishes, nor would it have applied during much of the eighteenth century, when Morning and Evening Prayer and the preaching of long sermons dominated Anglican worship, rather than the sacrament.

The inclusion of the use of the psalms in the list raises similar questions. Undoubtedly this has, descriptively, been an important part of Anglican worship, and was especially so when Matins and Evensong dominated the diet of worship in most parishes. But those days are many decades behind us now. In most Church of England parishes, the psalms are likely to be encountered mainly if there is a service of BCP Evening Prayer, and the number of parishes where this is a regular and well-attended service are getting fewer and fewer. In cathedrals it would be much easier to spot this as a defining feature of Anglican worship still, but not in most parish churches or chaplaincy situations. In many parishes, the only way the psalms are likely to be encountered with any regularity is if the songs or hymns which are sung draw upon the psalms – and even then, such connections are often tenuous. A hymn or song might be a paraphrase of a psalm, but more likely it will pick and mix verses or ideas from psalms, drawing inspiration but not necessarily much detailed content. What should we do then? Do we continue to assert the centrality of the psalms for Anglican worship *prescriptively*, hoping thereby to encourage their use? Or do we recognize *descriptively* that they are no longer a significant factor in worship in most Church of England churches, and cannot be part of any definition of Anglican worship?

Similar questions can be asked of the inclusion of the use of Collect prayers in the list. This has also been a part of historic Anglican worship, again deriving from the importance and prevalence of the Collect form of prayer in the services of Morning and Evening Prayer in the Prayer Book. But the dominance of eucharistic worship in the modern Church of England has altered how Collects are encountered: they are now chiefly experienced in the form of the Collect of the day, so that Collect prayers are increasingly seen as a 'theme' prayer for a service, rather than a form of prayer which can be used several times in a service in different contexts.

The Collect prayer in fresh expressions

There is a more significant question to be asked. If one is thinking about aspects of worship to urge upon a fresh expression of church as a key means of connecting with the wider Church of England and its worship, is it really the case that using a Collect is one of the crucial criteria? I suggest that if most pioneer ministers felt that using Collect prayers was a key part of the worship they were to lead and nurture in cutting-edge contexts of mission, they might just give up now.

As if all of this were not enough to make us realize the difficulty of the task, one can add the final problem, which is that some of the items on the list are notoriously open to interpretation. 'Form and dignity' are criteria which depend hugely on where one starts from and what one is comparing with. What one person calls 'dignity' another person might call 'dead formality', and yet another person might describe as slightly slapdash. Like beauty, it is in the eye of the beholder (or the ear of the worshipper).

The inclusion of the final point (economy of words) is similarly subjective. In the light of the massive *Common Worship* library, it is a point which sometimes strikes people as rather ironic, but in the context it refers not to the overall number of words in the liturgical resources of the Church of England, but to a care for liturgy in which particular forms or elements of worship aim to be rich but concise rather than verbose. A Eucharistic Prayer from *Common Worship* may not seem very concise to some ears, but when compared with some extempore prayer it can seem a model of concision. Context is everything when making these judgements.

More significantly, however, though it provides this list, the *Patterns for Worship* report also talks in terms of that broader sense of Anglican flavour which comes out in *The Hospitality of God*:

> 'Common Prayer' does not in fact exist, in the sense of being able to walk into any church in the land and find exactly the same words to follow. Nor should we pretend that it would be either good or right to return to a position – well over a century ago – when that might have been the case. Rather 'common prayer' exists in the Church of England in the sense of recognizing, as one does when visiting other members of the same family, some common features, some shared experiences, language and patterns or traditions. To accept a variety of forms, dictated by local culture, is part of our Anglican heritage . . .[25]

The Liturgical Commission go on to reflect on the danger of doctrinal error and the importance of doctrinal conformity – a key question if we are to move from a bounded to centred approach.

> Most debates about doctrinal conformity are really about how to stop the other person doing something you don't like because

---

25 *Patterns*, 1989, p. 5.

you think it is right on the edge of being heretical. We think the provisions of the Canons sufficiently safeguard this.[26]

They go on to quote Canon A5 which states that the doctrine of the Church of England 'is to be found in the Thirty-nine Articles of Religion, the *Book of Common Prayer*, and the Ordinal'. What they are effectively saying is, doctrine can be protected (and already is) by core texts and principles at the centre, rather than needing to be hedged around by specific worship texts at a boundary. This would have been a great place to stop. Unfortunately, they go on . . .

But we suggest, both to secure doctrinal orthodoxy and to avoid the divisions caused by 'party' texts, that there should be some parts of the service with a limited number of options.[27]

They recognize the contradiction between this and the idea of local creativity and local control, but they point to 'the traditional function of "catholic" faith and worship in providing a critique or alternative viewpoint for looking at local (or national) culture'.

Their point is right, but their proposed solution does not necessarily follow. You do not guarantee catholicity by fixing a boundary around certain texts: you work for catholicity by building in wider accountability. Child sacrifice is not an appropriate Christian form of all-age worship – but the reason we know this is not because it is not included in A Service of the Word!

Before we try to bring all of this together and draw some conclusions, we need to deal at greater length with that most slippery of concepts, which is so often quoted as being at the heart of Anglican understandings of worship: *lex orandi, lex credendi*.

---

26 *Patterns*, 1989, p. 6.
27 *Patterns*, 1989, p. 6.

Lex orandi, lex credendi

The Latin phrase *lex orandi, lex credendi* (law of praying, law of faith or believing) has a lot of weight placed on it in discussions of liturgy within the Church of England and the wider Anglican Communion. It is commonly asserted to be a standard Anglican principle, and so we need to pay some attention to it.

The phrase derives originally from a much longer passage by Prosper of Aquitaine, written in the fifth century. *Lex orandi, lex credendi* is taken as a simple summary of this longer passage, and is usually freely translated as something like, 'The law of praying establishes the law of believing', or more simply as, 'Worship establishes doctrine.' However, it can be taken to mean (or suggest) even more simply that prayer and worship are somehow intrinsically linked to our believing, rather than necessarily spelling out how that works.

Though it is often spoken of as an Anglican principle, it does not belong to the Church of England, neither does it find its origins there, nor is it part of official Anglican doctrine.

Just how 'Anglican' is *lex orandi, lex credendi*?

The phrase *lex orandi, lex credendi* could equally be said to be part of the understanding of worship in the Roman Catholic and Orthodox traditions, as well as in other Churches. The *Catechism of the Catholic Church* specifically refers to it in the section on the sacraments in the life of the Church, where it is taken in a fairly flexible way to refer to the intrinsic connection between liturgy and the Church's faith: 'the Church believes as she prays. Liturgy is a constitutive element of the holy and living Tradition.'[28]

The *lex orandi, lex credendi* epigram has been linked in the twentieth century with the growth in interest in liturgical

---

28 Roman Catholic Church, *Catechism of the Catholic Church*, London: Burns and Oates, revised edn, 1999, para. 1124, p. 258.

theology. Two of the key writers in this area are the Roman Catholic liturgist Aidan Kavanagh and the Orthodox theologian Alexander Schmemann.[29]

Kavanagh's approach (which has not gone unchallenged and is not shared by Schmemann) is to split liturgical theology into primary liturgical theology (the act of worship itself) and secondary liturgical theology (theological reflection on that activity). In that way, there is a two-way or, better, a circular pattern of action and reflection which allows belief and worship to critique one another, so that worship is able both to express and reinforce what we already believe about God, and also to shape how we might grow in understanding of God. It is not just the traditional mainstream denominations for whom this is the case. Writing from a non-denominational American evangelical perspective, Simon Chan is one of several arguing for worship's role in shaping belief, not in the sense of liturgical texts defining doctrine, but in the sense of the deep structures of worship shaping the Church's belief.[30]

In a Church of England context, what is usually being asserted is the idea that Anglican doctrine is located not in some confessional statement which needs to be signed up to, but in liturgical texts. This is made clear in the Preface to the Declaration of Assent, the declaration made by all authorized and licensed leaders of worship in the Church of England – clergy and Readers. There, in the list of the historic formularies of the Church of England, two out of the three are liturgical texts: *The Book*

---

29 See Aidan Kavanagh, *On Liturgical Theology*, New York: Pueblo, 1984, and Alexander Schmemann, *Introduction to Liturgical Theology*, trans. Asheleigh E. Moorhouse, Leighton Buzzard: Faith Press, 1975.

30 Simon Chan, *Liturgical Theology: The Church as Worshipping Community*, Downers Grove, IL: InterVarsity Press Academic, 2006, pp. 49f.

of Common Prayer and the Ordering of Priests and Deacons. The third is the Thirty-nine Articles of Religion.

However, *lex orandi, lex credendi* is something of a double-edged sword and can be a dangerous thing to invoke too boldly. As we have seen, in Anglican contexts the phrase is usually being read as: 'Our liturgical texts determine or show our doctrine.' In other words, if you want to know what Anglicans believe, look at how they pray – and how they pray is shaped by *The Book of Common Prayer*, and determined, even today, to a large degree centrally.

Angela Tilby is not untypical of this approach when she writes about 'that very important Anglican principle of *lex orandi lex credendi* (how the Church prays and worships tells us what it believes)'. She goes on, 'Until quite recently we have always been able to say that if you want to know what Anglicans *believe*, take part in our liturgical worship.'[31]

In summary, it is often used as a shorthand way of saying: for Anglicans, using some common liturgy (and especially, and certainly historically, using *The Book of Common Prayer*) is what establishes our belief and what makes us Anglican.

> Anglicans, asked what they believe, point not so much to a confession of faith as to a set of services . . . If there is not common prayer, there is a danger of a loss of common doctrine.[32]

Once you have established this as a determining principle (rather than as a mere fact of history) then any departure from the idea of common texts (and especially, from *these* common texts) is seen as un-Anglican and dangerous – it could lead us into . . . well, what exactly? Is there built into this the implication that departure from this pattern and these norms might lead us

---

31 Angela Tilby, 'What Questions Does Catholic Ecclesiology Pose for Fresh Expressions?', in Croft (ed.), *Mission-shaped Questions*, p. 82 (emphasis in original).

32 Michael Perham, 'Introduction', in Perham (ed.), *Renewal*, p. 5.

into unorthodoxy or even heresy? Or is it simply a fear that we might lose any sense of connection to our Anglican roots, albeit that we might still, in big-picture terms, be orthodox? Or is the fear more about a departure from 'Catholic' patterns and connections, understood to mean the Western tradition in a general sense, and therefore of the Church of England being less 'church' and more 'sect'? If that is the case, then it begs a question similar to the more focused one about what it is for worship to be Anglican: just how close would our worship need to be to other Churches, and to the Western tradition in particular, to still 'count' as Catholic?

Turning *lex orandi, lex credendi* back to front

The Latin can, however, be read another way: 'The ways that the Holy Spirit leads us to worship can and should influence how we understand God.' This has a very different implication. It suggests that if the worship which we have been given is no longer connecting with our culture, or if other ways of praying in Spirit and truth emerge, which are true to Scripture and to the historic Creeds (those other two key loci of Anglican doctrine), then they should allow us to question the beliefs, understanding and practice which have been handed down. This is effectively what many in fresh expressions of church are suggesting. Here's how Jonny Baker and Dean Ayres describe the process as it has emerged in the alternative worship congregation, Grace:

> Grace learns by doing. We do theology through the process of creating worship. That creates the context in which to discuss and draw on books and ideas in the tradition. We find we act our way into a new way of thinking rather than the other way round.[33]

---

33 Jonny Baker and Dean Ayres, *Making Communion: Grace Pocket Liturgies*, Proost – www.proost.co.uk, 2012, p. 14.

They are suggesting that those who are trying to engage with people outside the Church (whether through cafe church, or Goth church, or alternative worship, or other forms of fresh expression of church) and who are trying to find coherent and Scriptural ways of worshiping in those contexts, have new things to teach other parts of the Church about God. This, too, is *lex orandi, lex credendi*.

The truth is that *lex orandi, lex credendi* only sounds like an argument for keeping worship closely controlled when you have come from a context in which worship always *has* been closely controlled. Few suggest that we should apply the principle in the same way to the hymns and songs that are sung in the Church of England. These songs and hymns have also been passed on to us by the tradition (whether ancient or relatively recent), but this does not stop us wanting to critique them, or stop us living happily with the idea that different songs and hymns, and different styles and approaches, can be usefully and appropriately used in different contexts. No, it is the existence of printed liturgical books and the association of them with the uniformity sought by those in power at the time of the Reformation which makes us associate *lex orandi, lex credendi* with fixed forms of words, commonality and even uniformity, and with a particular Prayer Book or set of liturgical texts and their associated rules.

Lex orandi, lex credendi and the future of Anglican worship

So, let us sum up what we can say about where *lex orandi, lex credendi* fits into thinking about Anglican worship in the future:

- As a matter of sheer history, *lex orandi, lex credendi* has been part of Anglican thinking, when it is interpreted as saying, 'our fixed liturgical texts are what give us our doctrinal core'.

- The principle, however, is not, in essence, specifically Anglican.
- The principle has not, in Anglicanism, been applied to hymns and songs.
- The principle can be read and applied in a very different way, which suggests that the 'orandi' is a living Spirit-led tradition, which should be a motor for fresh understanding of God (within a scriptural and credal framework), not a fixed text which is a preserver of existing understandings of God and which becomes a self-perpetuating textual norm.

Does this mean that liturgical norms cannot any more be the way of defining what it is to be Anglican, and what it means to be Church of England in particular? That was certainly one of the conclusions of the International Anglican Liturgical Consultation meeting in York in 1989, in its statement 'Down to Earth Worship':

> Thus we believe that the Lambeth Resolutions . . . call in question attempts to identify Anglicanism, whether locally or worldwide, through any common liturgical texts, ethos or style. We believe the essential Anglican norms of Lambeth Resolution 47 are largely those contained within the Lambeth Quadrilateral and described within Lambeth resolution 18 – i.e. the Bible, Creeds, sacraments of the gospel, and episcopal ordination. We believe the use of vernacular language to be foundational to inculturation and within that value highly the 'traditional liturgical materials' to which Resolution 47 also refers. Our common liturgical heritage in items such as the Lord's Prayer promotes common prayer, sustains a dialogue with the scriptures, and conserves an element of the universal amid the particulars of inculturated worship.[34]

---

34 'The York Statement, "Down to Earth Worship"', in David R. Holeton (ed.), *Liturgical Inculturation in the Anglican Communion*, Alcuin/GROW Joint Liturgical Study 15, Nottingham: Grove Books, 1990, p. 12.

I think it might be time to acknowledge that the liturgical criterion was essentially about central control and power, and not about worship in Spirit and truth. That is not to say that there is no value in a connected way of thinking about worship – on the contrary – but it does mean that those patterns are better if they are predicated on principles of responsibility, trust and accountability, rather than on principles of law, conformity and uniformity, which we do not apply to other areas of church life. As Michael Moynagh puts it:

> When worship no longer has to carry the whole load of identity, belonging can be more inclusive and the tone of debates, perhaps, more generous. Not least, if worship need not carry the weight of denominational identity, gatherings can be freer to contextualize their worship.[35]

This recognition that liturgical norms may not be at the heart of Anglican identity any more can feel quite destabilizing. It is tempting to think that because in other areas of Anglican church life we cannot agree, therefore we need to unite around a liturgy which is the one thing which can hold us together. This can feel a little like the argument that the pews must not be removed from a church building because everything else in the community is changing and the church must be the one place where things stay constant.

Perhaps we need to be more confident and reliant on God rather than on particular forms of worship or even particular traditions and parts of tradition. The Anglican Churches of Africa have been wrestling with the same issue in the context of global Anglicanism, and they have concluded:

> Among Clergy and Laity alike there are many who fear change or fear losing their identity as Anglicans, or as members of a particular group within Anglicanism. May we all be open to the

---

35 Moynagh, *Church*, p. 372.

leading of God's Spirit and seek our security in the one whom we worship, rather than in the forms of worship themselves.[36]

It is not ultimately forms of liturgy that provide us with stability, but trust in a faithful God. This has also been recognized by the International Anglican Liturgical Consultation (IALC) in two of its meetings over recent decades (York in 1989 and Prague in 2005), which have looked at inculturation and at Anglican liturgical identity:

> The basic glue which holds us together as Anglicans is not the *Book of Common Prayer* nor even the spirit of the Prayer Book but, rather, our common will to live together as a communion of churches acting faithfully to proclaim the gospel among every people and culture.[37]

> Although within the [Anglican] Communion we are bound together by a common history, what really unites us, as with all Christians, is our one-ness in Christ through baptism and the Eucharist.[38]

Case Study

Prescriptive or descriptive?

I was giving a lecture on Anglican Liturgical Legalities, helping a group of students to engage with the history of Anglican

---

36 The Kanamai Statement, 1.1.iii, reproduced in David Gitari (ed.), *Anglican Liturgical Inculturation in Africa: The Kanamai Statement 'African Culture and Anglican Liturgy'*, Alcuin/GROW Joint Liturgical Study 28, Nottingham: Grove Books, 1994, p. 37.

37 David Holeton, 'Introduction', in Holeton (ed.), *Liturgical Inculturation*, p. 7.

38 'Appendix: Liturgy and Anglican Identity – A Discussion Document', in Irvine (ed.), *Anglican Liturgical Identity*, p. 46.

patterns of worship and some of the flexibility and the boundaries of *Common Worship*. As part of the lecture, we asked the question at the start of this chapter: 'What makes Anglican worship Anglican?' We began considering some of the lists that we have looked at in the chapter so far.

Eventually, one of the students put his hand up and said, in a rather frustrated way, 'You keep saying Anglican worship is this, and Anglican worship is that, but in my church it isn't any of these things, but we are still an Anglican church.' What he had put his finger on is a common dilemma when trying to use a label or to define a group of people. It is like defining an evangelical, or a Christian socialist. Do you proceed by reference to what those who have self-defined have said about themselves, or do you produce an objective list of criteria which may or may not apply to everyone who claims the label, and then refuse the label to those who do not fulfil all of them. This is the tension between descriptive and prescriptive definitions.

More significantly, the student was cutting the *lex orandi, lex credendi* knot. For him, his church is Church of England for reasons other than its worship (presumably structural and organizational reasons, such as how the leader is appointed, the fact that they pay a parish share to the diocese, how discipline is exercised, and so on). He defined his church as Anglican on the basis of relational and structural criteria, not liturgical or textual ones.

Bringing it all together

If we take an overview of the many different attempts to crystallize that illusive concept 'Anglican worship' which we have been exploring, we find that although different approaches are taken, there are common features, and these relate to the sorts of criteria which are applied. I summarize the different sorts of criteria in groups as follows:

1	Criteria to do with Anglican doctrinal foundations	As laid down in Canon A5 – Scripture, the Prayer Book, the Ordinal, and the Thirty-nine Articles.
2	Criteria to do with particular content for Anglican worship	The BCP, or other texts or aspects of content, which are taken as necessary or indicative of authentically Anglican worship; a sense of connectedness to a tradition in which commonality and a common Prayer Book have been important.
3	Criteria to do with an Anglican 'look and feel' for worship	Concepts such as 'dignity', 'beauty', 'reverence'; the value of some repetition and rhythm; congregational participation in spoken texts as well as song.
4	Criteria to do with current foci for Anglican worship – criteria 'of the moment'	Things which connect with current concerns in other areas of the Church's life (such as mission, or social justice).
5	Criteria to do with connections with other aspects of Anglican identity and values	The role of the bishop and connectedness with the wider Church; the importance of the local, contextual, vernacular and indigenous; the balance of ordained and lay in church government; a sense of responsibility for every part of the nation and the rights of parishioners to access the church and its worship; connection with the Lambeth Quadrilateral etc.

What we have here is a mixture of types of criteria. Some are quantitative and can be clearly measured in fairly objective ways. Others are qualitative and depend much more on interpretation and perspective.

Criteria to do with Anglican doctrinal principles

This heads our list because it is important to stress that the doctrinal core of Church of England worship is given clear shape and continued protection by the provisions of Canon A5, which spells out what the sources are for our doctrinal norms. These criteria are not only descriptive, they are prescriptive.

It should be noted that the BCP can still act as one of those doctrinal norms, even if it is not the required starting point for liturgical practice – that is, even if alternatives to BCP services were released from having to be approved centrally by General Synod and could be devised and approved more locally, involving the bishop.

Criteria to do with particular content for Anglican worship

Many of the attempts to narrow down what Anglican worship should look like include some aspects of particular content – the Lord's Prayer, the use of psalms, the use of Collect prayers, versicles and responses, and so on. This approach is an obvious starting point for determining Anglican criteria because of the dominance of the particular text, the BCP, in Anglican history, identity and liturgy.

The advantage of including these aspects is that they are much more concrete than the items that feature in some other rows of the table. These things are measurable and they start to show what the worship might actually look like. They give much clearer criteria for those tasked with producing services, or those who might have to apply 'the Anglican test'. However, the other side of that is that the more specific you are, the harder it becomes to find a list which is universally agreed. As descriptive features, the list can be fairly long; if we wish to make it a prescriptive list, then it needs to shrink considerably.

Further, we cannot escape the fact that many of these aspects of worship are not exclusively Anglican. The Lord's Prayer does not belong to us and, though its regular use in worship has been a feature of Anglican liturgy since Archbishop Cranmer, other Churches value it too. Responsive forms of liturgy similarly are not used solely in the Church of England, though there is a sense in which their regular and extended use, in the vernacular, with the aim of giving the people a voice in the liturgy, was discovered as a powerful tool by the Church of England at its founding.

These content criteria, however, do help to put some flesh on the bones of what has historically been part of the resources which the Church of England has provided. Though they may not work as 'must have' lists, they provide a good indicative list of the sort of thing that one might expect to be part of worship in the Church of England family – not every aspect will be present in every act of worship, but one might expect there to be a good *reason* why not, rather than for it simply to have been overlooked or ignored.

A more helpful way forward may be to put services and forms of worship which have been or are authorized or commended as part of what goes at the centre, and to let people recognize the parts of the heritage which connect with their situation. This might mean taking a longer-term view – rather than counting, 'Is there the Lord's Prayer, or a Creed, or a confession, in this service?' we might ask, 'Is the Lord's Prayer being used regularly in public worship, often enough for people to get to know it by heart? Is a Creed used often enough for worshippers to be familiar with it? Is someone looking at the long-term pattern of hymns and songs which are sung to see if there is a doctrinal balance or if the focus is skewed unhelpfully? Is confession a regular part of worship for all worshippers, whichever service they come to most regularly?'

Criteria about 'Look and feel'

Several of the attempts above include some sort of 'qualitative' assessment of worship as part of what makes it properly 'Anglican'. Words such as 'form', 'dignity', 'reverence', beauty' are notoriously difficult to pin down. More importantly, they are not exclusive to Anglican worship. I would expect that a Roman Catholic document on liturgy, or an Orthodox one, would also talk about the dignity and beauty of worship. Nonetheless, the choice of adjectives is telling, and does say something about how at least some Anglicans have understood the core values of worship.

A bigger question is begged though: 'Are these the right words to describe what Church of England worship *should* "look and feel" like?' Some other churches (both in the sense of denominations, and in the sense of local congregations, even in the Church of England) might choose a different set of adjectives: lively, Spirit-filled, welcoming, warm, informal, spontaneous. It is one thing to say that reverent and dignified describes how worship often has been, it is another to say that it prescribes the key features that we should aspire to in every Anglican act of worship. They clearly apply to most cathedral worship, and much 'traditional' Church of England worship, but are they the key words to apply to worship in fresh expressions of church, or at the toddler service, or even at the monthly all-age worship service? It is not that they are bad things to aspire to, simply that they may not be the *priority* terms to aim for in particular contexts. Accessibility might take precedence over dignity in some contexts; flexibility might be more important than form in some others; sometimes beauty will be of the popular sort, not the high art sort; at times it matters more that we offer *our* best, rather than somebody's concept of *the* best.

So the 'look and feel' criterion starts to look as if it matters in terms of seeing some historical family likeness, but it needs interpreting and adapting for new situations and particular circumstances. If we are saying 'worship should be done well, with care and attention' then that is probably a more helpful way to put it, which leaves open the question of what 'doing it well' looks like in a particular situation. It means that we recognize that worship should reflect the best that we can do, it should include a sense of giving something costly which has taken effort and energy, and it should be about going for the maximum not the minimum. It cannot, in the mixed context of the current Church of England, mean worship which is 'always perfect' by some external standard. It can therefore function as a descriptive set of criteria in so far as it describes how that desire for 'doing it well' has been enacted in the past, but it needs to be carefully phrased if it is to become a prescriptive feature of Church of England worship today.

All of this means that we have a criterion which is about recognizing worship as a key aspect of the Church's mission and life, which deserves to have time and energy spent on it, and which needs resourcing both in terms of short-term content and in the longer-term aspects of training for leaders and so on. But this makes it a generic criterion which we share with other Churches: we are simply saying, 'Worship should look and feel as if it matters.' That's helpful, and important to put at the 'centre', but it needs other criteria alongside it to focus it down. As a criterion it is useful, but not sufficient.

Criteria about a current focus

Several of the lists we have looked at include things which are seen as important in worship because they reflect things which are important in the wider Church. The most obvious example is the focus on worship's part in mission, to be outward looking and to be part of the Church's calling to welcome others to worship God in Christ. This includes the practical implications that worship should be welcoming and accessible. In one sense this seems self-evident, but it is important to recognize that this is a particular emphasis in the wider life of the Church and though there have always been those who recognize its importance, it would not be true to say that it has always been a focus of the Church of England as a whole.

There are other examples: a look at the liturgical texts of the ASB, or the songs and hymns that were being written at the time, shows important theological or ecclesiological emphases, which began to manifest themselves in the text or structures of the Church's worship: a recovery of a sense of the importance

of the Trinity as a doctrine at the heart of Christian understanding of God; the recovery of a lively expectation of the
role of the Holy Spirit in bringing faith to life, pointing us to
Christ and equipping and empowering us for Christian living;
the image of the Church as Body of Christ or as family.

Perhaps the equivalent theological shift in worship today is the
growing recognition of the importance of a strong and clear theology of creation, with its implications for our understanding of
God, of our planet and our responsibilities towards it, of other
human beings made in God's image, and of the role of human-
kind in relation to other parts of the created order. This emphasis
is also being picked up in worship and is an emphasis which many
would wish to see at the heart of the Church's worship too.

These sorts of criteria are also not exclusive to the Church of
England; we share them with many other Christians. However,
they are not necessarily shared equally by every local congregation, and that is where there is something about the Church of
England's ecclesiology and way of determining worship that
is, if not exclusive, then certainly distinctive compared to at
least some Churches, and that is the role of the wider Church
(expressed through things like centrally produced liturgical
resources, questions asked in archdeacons' visitations etc.), to
be prophetic and to ask challenging questions of local churches
and their worship. The Church of England is not congregational in its structures nor in its approach to worship; the local
is accountable to the whole, and the whole can expect a role in
critiquing and challenging what takes place locally.

In terms of a centred-set approach, this would be a changing part of the centre, which might be prescriptive in terms of
the principles it enunciates, but it would need to be regularly
reviewed to allow for new foci and fresh emphases to develop. It
is, however, important, because it recognizes the important role
the wider Church has in setting criteria which are not necessarily the priorities of local churches but which ought to be taken
into account: so, whether mission is your first thought when it
comes to worship or not, the wider Church requires you to consider it; whether ecological issues and care for the environment

are things your vicar cares about passionately or not, the wider Church can ask you what you are doing to engage with those issues in worship, and can provide resources to help.

Criteria to do with other aspects of Anglican identity, applied to worship

Here we return to Steven Croft's suggested focus on Anglican values. These need to be concrete principles which are widely agreed on, but not so widely as to become the liturgical equivalent of 'Mom and apple pie'. Taking Croft's suggestion of the Chicago-Lambeth Quadrilateral plus the Five Marks of Mission, and focusing on expanding the liturgical aspects of these, we might include things like:

- Episcopal leadership and the importance of the bishop as a focus for unity, and the primary minister, evangelist and pastor of the diocese. Equally we might see the bishop as the primary liturgical leader of the diocese, taking overall responsibility for the worship of the diocese, and for its connection with wider Church of England norms. Bishops might delegate some of that authority to appropriate advisors, just as they do in other areas of their responsibilities, where their own expertise lies elsewhere.
- Synodical government as a symbol and outworking of the principle of sharing leadership and governance between lay and ordained. At congregational level, that would imply the involvement of the PCC and other representatives of the laity in worship decisions, not just the vicar and her or his latest bright ideas.
- The importance of leadership which is recognized beyond the local, including leadership which is appointed from outside. This would include the threefold order of ordained ministry, but also the importance of Readers or Licensed Lay Ministers of various sorts, the expectation that those who preach regularly will have undergone some training

and will be licensed in some way which puts them beyond the whim of the incumbent, the idea that others who are not directly called, trained and appointed are accountable to those who are, so that, for instance, leaders of worship bands, or organists and choir leaders, operate under the authority of the incumbent and, via the incumbent, of the bishop.

- A concern for context (including the parish system), and being true to a particular place and time.

- The concern for mission and ministry which is for all people, whether they see themselves as naturally religious and are churchgoers, or not. In England that is part of the responsibility of being the Established Church – parishioners have rights (e.g. to marriage in the parish church, to baptism or to the funeral rites of the Church) depending on their residency or sometimes on other connections with the church, but those rights are not generally dependent on attendance, regular financial giving, voting rights, etc. This means that we do not give ourselves the luxury of just 'doing our own thing' on the understanding that people can go elsewhere if they want something else – for us, that is not an option.

- Ecumenism – part of our self-understanding is that we are not the Church, we are part of the Church. Covenanted relationships should be important to us and have implications for worship. This understanding should also relativize our claims about the importance of our particular tradition in terms of its specifics, even if we recognize its value historically, and the possibility, but not the inevitability, of it having ongoing usefulness and value for the future. An awareness of our contingency entails a willingness to die (including liturgically). If we genuinely say we have no particular doctrines but those which have been held by all Christians, can we also say that in some sense we also have no particular liturgical emphases other than those which have been recognized as valuable in all Christian traditions. It also leads us to another question: 'How is what we do true to what the wider Church beyond us is doing?' The answer will remind us of the importance of working ecumenically, using agreed texts in worship where we can, and so on.

These are less easily measurable than simple elements of the textual content of worship, but as principles they ought to be prescriptive as aspirations for Anglican worship.

Vital but not sufficient

None of these criteria or sets of criteria will be sufficient on their own to define in a watertight way that an act of worship has been properly 'Church of England'. What we have is a list of properties of Anglican worship, rather than a single defining property. It is the combination which helps us to discern authentically Anglican worship. Taken together, they provide a good set of criteria against which worship which calls itself Church of England can be evaluated and by which leaders of such worship can make themselves accountable to the wider Church. If none of these criteria are addressed by a congregation's worship (or very few, and very few of the more specific and concrete ones) then we have every right to ask whether the worship, good and helpful as it may have been, can legitimately be said to be an act of worship of the Church of England. If some of these criteria are addressed by a worshipping congregation, then we might be able to see the worship as authentically Anglican, even if some other elements which have historically been typical of Anglican worship are not present in a particular service.[39]

---

39 I am grateful to Dr Kate Distin for pointing out the parallels here with the taxonomy of viruses, which is different from other forms of biological taxonomy, being more 'fuzzy' and less clearly bounded. In biological terms this is helpful when trying to categorize things which vary considerably and undergo constant evolutionary change. I hesitate to call Church of England worship 'viral' ...

What we have here, then, is the beginnings of a collection of things which we can put at the centre of our centred set, things towards which we might expect Church of England worship to 'tend' or to move, or at which we might expect it to point.

5

Some Implications of a
Centred-Set Approach

So, what else would this different centred-set approach mean?

1 New Canons

The reason that a new approach would require some revision of
the Canons of the Church of England is the commitment made
by all clergy and licensed Readers that they will use only forms
of worship 'authorized or allowed by canon'. The restrictions
that surround the *Common Worship* services are not primarily the result of *Common Worship* itself, but of the canonical
framework within which *Common Worship* sits.

A new approach would require complementary Canons which
stop setting boundaries and start focusing on what is at the
centre. Instead of Canon B5 allowing for local decision *only*
where there is no authorized service, it might be rewritten to
allow for local decision for any form of service and any aspect
of services, as long as it is reverent and seemly and not contrary
to Church of England doctrine. Effectively, it would be making all centrally produced services 'commended services' – ones
which are commended by the House of Bishops as appropriate
for Church of England worship – reverent and seemly and so
on.

Instead of the Canons about worship specifying what you can
and cannot do, they could focus on who you need to consult
with when determining worship at a local level. So: if you want

to change the pattern of services the Canons might require you to consult with the PCC; if you want to use locally composed Eucharistic Prayers you would need to inform the bishop or consult with his diocesan liturgical advisory group, and so on.

There is also scope for applying the same approach (centred rather than bounded) to the Canons which relate to such matters as the vesture of ministers at services. But this would not just be about rolling *back* canon law – there is a good case for *extending* the ideas enshrined in it (loyalty to doctrinal norms etc.) to hymns and songs, which probably have a greater impact on worshippers than any spoken liturgy.[1]

Canon law revision

There is likely to be little enthusiasm in General Synod for any large-scale canon law revision. When the canons were revised wholesale in the 1950s under Archbishop Geoffrey Fisher, there were many in the Church of England who were frustrated by the length of the process and disappointed with the results.[2] However, it was this revision which set the scene for some of the problems which we are now having to work through.

The key decision then was to make the new Canons a revision of the Canons of 1604. This meant a lot of modernizing and taking account of fresh contexts, but the overall shape of the Canons, and the basic ethos was unchanged: a very large number of very detailed Canons, which give the Church of

---

1 A point made by Kenneth Stevenson in 'Anglican Identity and Church of England Worship Today: An Historical Reflection', in Michael Perham (ed.), *The Renewal of Common Prayer: Unity and Diversity in Church of England Worship* (GS Misc 412), London: Church House Publishing SPCK, 1993, p. 13. See also, Christopher Irvine and Anders Bergquist, 'Thinking about Liturgy', *Anaphora* 5:2 (2011), p. 54.

2 For more on this, see Andrew Chandler and David Hein, *Archbishop Fisher, 1945–1961: Church, State and World*, Farnham: Ashgate, 2012, pp. 50–4.

England's governance a very bureaucratic and technical feel. They focus the role of bishops on being authority figures who make sure rules are kept, rather than on being senior pastors and overseers who have the flexibility to work with local clergy to devise appropriate strategy (and worship) for the particular contexts.

Some had hoped for a different approach altogether, which started from questions about what was required now, rather than taking the existing Canons as the starting point. Had Archbishop William Temple still been alive, the approach might have been different, as he had little time for 'mechanical uniformity' in relation to canon law, preferring an approach focusing on loyalty rather than legalism. An approach like that might have given us a looser, less detailed structure of canon law, a structure based more on trust than on legal detail.

For now, we have the Canons we have. What is suggested here is not a wholesale revision of canon law, but a careful look at those most clearly focused on worship with a view to revising them in a direction which looks for trust in those who lead local churches, coupled with a clear line of accountability for those local decisions. See Appendix 2 for some initial suggestions.

2   New urgency for liturgical training for leaders

This is already desperately urgent. I consider myself fortunate to have one of the few full-time liturgical teaching jobs in the Church of England's theological courses and colleges. It is telling that the national role of Worship Development Officer for the Church of England (a post which was only instituted less than ten years ago) has been reduced from full-time to effectively quarter-time.

This liturgical training and foundation-building becomes more important, not less, as more and more Church of England churches embrace informal styles of worship, and as fresh expressions of church become more common. It is tempting to suggest that those being trained for pioneer ministries should spend more time focusing on contemporary issues, contextual and inculturated forms of worship, and be spared some of the more historical material and an understanding of different historical traditions. However, if they are to be equipped with the tools to critique contemporary trends and to contextualize in ways which have integrity with the Christian tradition, then the historical understanding of Christian worship in different times and places becomes more important than ever. Historical patterns provide a mirror which can be held up to modern approaches to help us to see ourselves in a wider context and to ask the questions of our assumptions that those from other times and places might ask.

If we were to take on a centred-set approach, we would be acknowledging that you get good worship by selecting and training the right people, not by making the right rules. We would need people who know how to be both loyal and creative. Rather than trying to cut out improvisation, we would need to train people how to improvise well on an 'Anglican' theme. Adrian Chatfield has helpfully summed up what is at stake:

> I remain unconvinced that pioneering requires a rejection of ancient traditions. What is much truer to a religion built on memory, it seems to me, is deep understanding of the patterns and reasons for those traditions, accompanied by significant experience of the ancient practice. Then, and only then, can it be adapted (and occasionally rejected) in modern settings and fresh expressions. New church and worship leaders need to engage in double listening – to the people among whom they live and to the inheritance of the church of God.[3]

Perhaps the most significant part of this is his emphasis on the need for 'significant experience of the ancient practice'.

---

3 Adrian Chatfield, 'Form and Freedom: Creating Pioneering Worship', in Dave Male (ed.), *Pioneers 4 Life: Explorations in Theology and Wisdom*, Abingdon: BRF, 2011, p. 122.

Authentic improvisation on a theme relies on thorough knowledge of the theme.

On top of the need to train local liturgical leaders, it would also be important to train and prepare those who would be part of the accountability structures which would be necessary to balance the powers of the leaders of the services themselves. This might include Parochial Church Councils or other localized groups.

The 1991 report, *The Worship of the Church as it Approaches the Third Millennium*, includes a section asking why we have a centralized procedure for authorizing worship in the Church of England. It continues:

> Is it to ensure that unsuspecting laity do not have unsuitable liturgies thrust upon them by romanizing or ultra-charismatic clergy? To give PCCs more power over the whole of worship (the contents as well as the rite . . .) might be a better way of achieving this than debating details in Synod: but is it possible to work out a way of giving a PCC some say over the 'style' and general contents, without a PCC tyranny over each individual prayer?[4]

It raises here an interesting question, which is how localized decision-making can also be balanced, just as national decision-making has been balanced, to make sure that particular individuals, or committees, do not have all the power.

3   A new role for bishops in their dioceses

For an episcopally led Church, surely this should be part of the answer? A Diocesan Liturgical Committee could become an advisory group to the bishop for these sorts of situations.

---

4 Church of England: Liturgical Commission, *The Worship of the Church as it Approaches the Third Millennium* (GS Misc 364), London: Church House Publishing, 1991, pp. 20f., para. 68.

This will sound quite dangerous to some, no doubt. 'What about bishops that know nothing about liturgy?' I hear you ask. But we already leave one of the most significant aspects of developing ministry and mission in bishops' hands – the decision about how the ordained and licensed leadership of churches is handed on. As someone working in a theological college I am very conscious of the bishops' role in deciding whom they will ordain. The reports I prepare are to make recommendations to bishops about ordination, but they can and do overturn those recommendations – sometimes advisedly, sometimes not. And of course, in practice they are advised by Diocesan Directors of Ordinands, vocation advisers, Bishops' Advisory Panels, course and college reports and others.

In liturgical terms, we could work the same way. The bishop might have the final say, but would work with others and be advised, perhaps, by their diocesan liturgical committees. We have already seen that people who want to do creative things in worship, which are not allowed under current rules, instinctively look to the bishop to say 'okay' or to allow them to be 'experimental', and bishops instinctively think they can give that sort of permission. Perhaps it is time to let them do so. This would be the result of allowing bishops more discretion to apply dispensations, to apply my suggested Bishops' Liturgical Orders and Local Liturgical Projects.

The suggestion of this book, however, is that maybe it is time to let them do more than that, to let them be not just liturgical permission-givers but active agents of liturgical renewal, working with clergy and lay leaders to discern what might be culturally relevant but connected with the wider tradition in particular contexts within their dioceses. In this way, they could be innovators, not just gate-keepers, and church leaders could feel that going to seek help from the bishop would not be about what you could get away with, but what the bishop might encourage you to try out.

An example from Southern Africa

In the Anglican Church of Southern Africa, it is now possible for a diocesan bishop to give authorization for culturally appropriate forms of worship, as long as they are 'consistent with the doctrines and discipline of the Church'.[5]

4 A new role for the Liturgical Commission

What is the Liturgical Commission for?

The Church of England has only had a standing Liturgical Commission since the mid-1950s, though there were earlier, short-lived committees concerned with particular aspects of liturgical revision. It was set up as part of the long-term response to the failure of the proposed 1928 Prayer Book to secure parliamentary approval. The Church of England began to look at ways to take the control of liturgical revision more fully into its own hands. The Liturgical Commission was the body set up by the Convocations of Canterbury and York, and initially appointed by the Archbishops in 1955, to do the work of producing alternative services.

Initially it was a commission of experts in liturgical theology and history, charged with producing alternative services which took into account the key traditions of the Church as well as the latest liturgical thinking which was coming out of the Liturgical Movement.

---

5 Cynthia Botha, 'Worship and Anglican Identity – A Resume', in Christopher Irvine (ed.), *Anglican Liturgical Identity: Papers from the Prague Meeting of the International Anglican Liturgical Consultation*, Alcuin/Grow Joint Liturgical Studies 65, Norwich: Canterbury Press, 2008, p. 17.

The Liturgical Commission is still appointed by the arch-bishops, acting on advice from the General Synod Appointments Committee. Nowadays, the chair is always a bishop, because the Liturgical Commission is, constitutionally, an advisory body to the House of Bishops. It takes its instructions for the work it does from the House of Bishops, and always delivers that work to the House of Bishops in the first instance. If General Synod asks for a piece of work to be done, it does so by requesting the House of Bishops to ask the Liturgical Commission to do it, and the work, when it is done, comes back to General Synod for discussion, revision or final approval via the House of Bishops again.

But it has increasingly become a *representative* commission rather than merely an expert commission. Its members are drawn from General Synod itself, supplemented by others who have particular areas of expertise. The Commission members appointed in this way then seek others to work with them as consultants, and added into the mix are co-opted members (such as the chaplain to General Synod) and those appointed from other Churches (such as the Roman Catholic Church and the Methodist Church) to act as observers. The final group sitting round the table can easily consist of 25 people, some of whom have particular liturgical knowledge or skills, but some of whom have been chosen from General Synod because they represent other important voices in the process, such as youth or music, or cathedrals or parishes or Readers and so on.

For most of its existence, the major part of the Liturgical Commission's work has been producing various alternative services – from Series 1, Series 2 and Series 3, right through to the *Alternative Service Book 1980*, the seasonal and other resources which followed and supplemented it, and the *Common Worship* materials which ultimately replaced it.

Since 2006, the Liturgical Commission agenda has been focused not so much on textual work, but on 'liturgical formation' – how to improve the practice and understanding of worship at local level.[6] However, the problem with the Commission trying to do formational work is that, no matter how hard it tries, it is seen by others as the liturgical thought police, 'checking up on people's worship'. The reason that this impression is so hard to shake off is that it is very hard to focus on formation in a system which is built on boundaries. When everyone is scared of doing it wrong, they don't ask for help, and the Liturgical Commission (as much because of that intimidating title as anything else) are seen as oppressors rather than advisors. Among the current Liturgical Commission there is something of a recognition of this problem, and this has led to the Commission turning once again to Praxis in the hope of using its 'semi-official, off-shore' nature to make formation feel more collaborative and less threatening.

A new centred-set future for Church of England liturgy might mean a revised role for a national Liturgical Advisory Commission. Its agenda might include:

- The production of **texts** which are deemed to represent 'good practice' but which don't have to be considered *essential* – effectively 'commended services' for everything, but in a variety of styles and to suit different contexts.
- The production of **guidelines** for good practice – for instance over inclusive language and expansive language, or over the use of technology in worship.
- **Advising** the House of Bishops, and maybe individual bishops, on liturgical matters, including matters relating to worship in fresh expressions of church and pioneering contexts.

---

6 In fact, this was being suggested way back in 1991 in the report, *The Worship of the Church as it Approaches the Third Millennium*, p. 25, para 84.

Possible politicization

One of the dangers of giving a more directive role to diocesan liturgical committees (by expecting them to advise diocesan bishops), Praxis regions and the national Liturgical Commission is that the question of who serves on these groups becomes more likely to attract attention and controversy. While these groups have a limited role, no one worries too much about who serves on them (the exception being the Liturgical Commission, because of its role in producing draft liturgical texts). If, however, your local experimental communion service has to be 'checked out' by the diocesan liturgical committee before the bishop will give permission for you to use it, then suddenly everyone becomes more interested in who serves on that committee, how they are chosen, and so on. Perhaps there would be pressure to elect people to these positions. That in turn raises questions about whether these groups should be primarily chosen for their expertise or skills, or for their ability to represent different groups and traditions within the Church. These are undoubtedly important questions, but they ought not to be reasons not to consider making the changes suggested here.

Case Study

All-age Eucharist at St Philip's – in a different world

Paula had been in post as Vicar of St Philip's Church for six months and was turning her mind to how to 'attract more families and children to church' – something that the advert for her post had said the PCC were enthusiastic about.

She met with a small sub-group of the PCC, and they decided to suggest a bold new pattern of worship, which extended their provision of all-age worship. There was already a non-eucharistic all-age service on the first Sunday in the month, but they were keen to make the Eucharists on the other

Sundays of the month all-age as well. The non-eucharistic all-age service was very informal and had been growing over the previous few years, so Paula was keen to make sure that the eucharistic services were not a huge jump for those who had become worshippers at the monthly all-age service but had never really come to any other services.

She remembered some creative liturgies, which also seemed child-friendly, which she had encountered when she trained for ordination, and she reached for them now on her shelves. She found one that seemed to fit the informality she was looking for, and which would not need very much adapting to the particular circumstances at St Philip's. Her first thought was to talk with her bishop.

The bishop was delighted to get her letter and forwarded a copy to the Diocesan Liturgical Committee. This was just the sort of creative, outward-focused approach to worship that he was trying to encourage in the diocese. Because Paula wanted to use material which was not in *Common Worship*, she needed to give an account of her reasons and to get some training in informal patterns of eucharistic presidency. The Diocesan Liturgical Committee offered courses for those in situations like this, making sure clergy had a good grounding in the history of patterns of Eucharistic Prayers and were aware of some of the doctrinal issues which were particularly significant in the Church of England. The Committee appointed a consultant from their number who would work with Paula and her PCC sub-group to produce material for their all-age Eucharists and who would give some feedback and suggestions for good practice. Paula was also put in touch with two other churches in the diocese which had recently done a similar thing. The bishop would then be asked to give his approval for the material to be used for six months. After that, Paula would be asked to give a brief report on how things were going and on any changes she intended to make. The bishop might then give a further year's permission for the material to be used.

Some risks

Is it inevitable that creativity at congregational level will mean that English Anglicans can no longer feel at home in different parish churches? Must the sensitive adaptation of worship to local culture lead to the formation of personal patterns of devotion that are more parochial than national or catholic? Are liturgical anarchy and the fragmentation of personal spirituality an inevitable result of increasing deregulation of public worship?[7]

These are some of the questions that may be provoked by the ideas in this book, but they were originally questions raised by Michael Vasey when writing on behalf of the Liturgical Commission during the time between the ASB and CW. The questions, in other words, already exist, provoked by the diversity we already have in Church of England worship – they are not suddenly raised by the suggestions being made here.

There are risks, of course, in moving from a bounded to a centred approach. It is the desire to avoid risk and a basic lack of trust in one another which moves us to legislate, so a different model based less on legislation and more on trust is bound to involve a greater degree of risk. We may have to risk getting it wrong – or other people getting it 'wrong'.

Some will worry that a different approach would mean the Roman Missal being used in lots of Anglican churches. If so, it will be no different from now. Would *more* Church of England parishes use it than do so now? I doubt it. And the centred approach would still provide grounds on which to question it and to hold worship leaders accountable.

'Or,' some will say, 'more churches would abandon robes and do nothing but sing songs and preach and offer prayer ministry.' Would they? It's possible, and many already do. But if it is unhelpful, the best way to stop it is to show why it is

---

7 Michael Vasey, 'Promoting a Common Core', in Perham (ed.), *Renewal*, p. 82.

unhelpful and what it misses out, not to make a rule banning it. On the whole, however, I suspect a change would not affect the number of churches doing this. Those that consider it important in their context are, generally speaking, already doing it, whatever the Church's rules say. In any case, part of the problem for many evangelical and charismatic Anglicans is not that they are opposed to liturgy as such, they just see liturgy as something that stops them listening to the Spirit themselves – let liturgy be their own idea and I wouldn't be surprised if they do not start using it *more*, as other evangelicals are (for example, in some Vineyard Churches).

For others, the fear might be that *The Book of Common Prayer* will be used even less. Again, I suggest that there would be little or no effect here. At the local level, there is already a choice about how much the Prayer Book is used for services. What the centred-set approach makes explicit is that the important place of the Prayer Book *for* all within the Church of England does not depend upon its regular use *by* all within the Church of England. We have already learned to live with this reality.

And in all of this, of course, we should not forget that there are questions to be asked about our current system of authorizing liturgies via a complex process of committees and discussion in full sessions of General Synod. Things have improved a lot, but the results of the current process are often still more to do with church politics than with good liturgical principles, wise liturgical creativity or rich liturgical language. The phrase 'herding cats' has been heard to be applied to the process on many occasions.

The death of common prayer?

As we have seen, perhaps the greatest fear for some would be that the approach suggested here would mean the death of 'common prayer' altogether as an Anglican concept. Here I turn to the 1991 report of the Liturgical Commission, *The Worship of the Church as it Approaches the Third Millennium*, which points out that carol services are probably the most predictable form of common prayer known in England (certainly in the Church of England), and yet there is no control over them, because they are not an authorized form of service.[8] Some people do very creative things with them, they can change organically in response to changes in society, but there is at the centre a clear core (and between them a family likeness), which means that you know when you have been to one. What is more, people are not afraid to critique things which are advertised as carol services but which do not seem to produce what the description suggests.

What this reminds us is that commonality is a concept which does not depend on control or enforcement. Anglicans assume that it does because that is how we have experienced it in relation to our liturgical texts.

Commonality is also a concept which begs a question: 'In common with whom?' There are a range of possible answers:[9]

- Other Church of England churches.
- Other churches in your locality, of different denominations.
- Other churches in your country, of different denominations.
- Other Anglican churches around the world.
- English-speaking churches of other denominations around the world.

A glance back at the history of worship over the last sixty years or so reminds us that at the same time as worship in the Church of England has got gradually more diverse in terms of liturgical texts, in the bigger picture of Christian worship in England

---

8 *The Worship of the Church as it Approaches the Third Millennium*, p. 10, para 23.

9 Mark Earey, Perran Gay and Anne Horton, *Understanding Worship: A Praxis Study Guide*, London: Mowbray, 2001, p. 22.

there has been a growing commonality.[10] If we look at hymnody and songs, we will probably find a greater commonality in repertoire than ever before across churches of different denominations and between churches of different traditions within a denomination. This is partly because the ecumenical movement has made us more aware of the treasures in each other's traditions, but it is also because the technology of desktop publishing, the internet and data projectors has released us from the grip of denominational hymnbooks, so that we can source our musical repertoire from a greater range of resources.

Within the Church of England the growing dominance of the Eucharist as a main Sunday service in churches of evangelical as well as central or catholic tradition has brought more commonality to Sunday morning worship than existed previously. From the other end of the spectrum, the growth in 'family services', and all-age worship, which began in more evangelical parishes, has now also influenced more catholic parishes, albeit that the all-age worship is more likely to be an all-age Eucharist in the latter.

People increasingly choose their church on a whole range of criteria which do not always include denominational affiliation, such as the provision of children's activities or the musical style or approach to small groups or preaching. This means that Anglican congregations include those whose worship DNA contains a whole range of expectations and commonalities which are not necessarily to do with the historic worship patterns or texts of the Church of England.

So, in part we are looking at the end of a control-focused commonality to Anglican worship, but that is not the same as saying we would end any commonality. Certainly the wider commonalities we have noted would continue, and the centred approach

---

10 For more on this, see Donald Gray, 'An Ecumenical Approach to Common Prayer', in Perham (ed.), *Renewal*, pp. 44–54. He particularly notes that the Church of Scotland, as an established Church with a *Book of Common Order*, does not take the same approach to controlling commonality as the Church of England.

advocated here would provide a different sort of commonality, not focused so much on particular worship texts but on being a Church gathered around some particular approaches, doctrinal norms, historic forms of service, and inherited patterns, and with particular patterns of accountability.

Accountability

One of the crucial steps in taking away a boundaried approach to liturgy is to make sure that a centred approach brings with it a clear sense of broader accountability for liturgy in local churches, so that the Church of England retains a sense of being a connexional, rather than congregational, Church.

It ought to be possible to ask of any local act of worship that takes place in the Church of England questions which hold it accountable to the wider Church. The concept of worship audit or liturgical consultancy is already around in the Church and has been promoted and offered by diocesan liturgical committees for many years.[11] Often it is part of a wider mission audit or of the process of mission action planning. It would not be a huge shift to formalize this so that the evaluation of worship was not just an occasional choice made at local level, but a regular expectation, backed up by diocesan or national resources and coupled to a process of external (but friendly) accountability.

At the level of foundational principles, these might be good questions to ask of any Church of England act of worship:[12]

---

11 See, for instance, Mark Earey, *Worship Audit: Making Good Worship Better*, Grove Worship Series 133, Nottingham: Grove Books, 1995. The Liturgical Commission's 2007 report, *Transforming Worship: Living the New Creation* (GS1651), also stresses the value of worship audit (pp. 26–7).

12 These are drawn and adapted from principles of inculturation applied to the Roman Catholic post-Vatican 2 'Mass for Zaire', quoted in Phillip Tovey, *Inculturation: The Eucharist in Africa*, Alcuin/GROW Joint Liturgical Studies 7, Nottingham: Grove Books, 1988, p. 35.

- Does it exhibit faithfulness to the gospel (i.e. to all the big-picture material about what makes worship good – connected with theology and doctrine, full of good news, open to all, and so on)?
- Does it exhibit faithfulness to the Church's historic liturgy, as the Church of England has received and adapted it historically (i.e. connections to BCP and other patterns which have been important, as conversation partners and mirrors to our contemporary practice)?
- Does it exhibit faithfulness to the cultural context for which this worship is intended (i.e. to the people and place in which the worship will be offered)?

Ian Tarrant has suggested a further series of questions which would be good starting points in any accountability process:[13]

- Is this worship in keeping with the faith of the Church of England?
- Is the worship here likely to bring the church into disrepute in any way?
- Are God's people being nurtured in their spiritual growth and service?
- Have church members been consulted and involved in the planning?

These questions cover process (such as the involvement of others in planning worship and making decisions about it) as well as content, and keep our eyes on the overall aim.

The key would be to think about how and where and when such questions could be asked. Perhaps they could be part of an archdeacon's visitation, or a regular item on a PCC agenda or for the support group for a pioneer minister to ask.

---

13 Ian Tarrant, *Worship and Freedom in the Church of England*, Cambridge: Grove Books, 2012, p. 16.

Making the rules worshipper-focused rather than institution-focused

One of the problems with *Common Worship* that we explored earlier was the problem caused by the idea of a principal service, which determines so much of the boundaries and freedoms for planning a service. Ian Tarrant suggests that the problem with the principal service idea is that it is focused on the institution and the rules, rather than focused on the experience of actual worshippers. One could fulfil the letter of the law with regard to the rules, but end up with worship which fails to fulfil the spirit of the law with regard to actual worshippers. Tarrant suggests a series of guideline questions for a church to ask itself, which are focused on what the worshippers experience, rather than on what the church provides:

Some worshipper-focused guidelines[14]

Every church member should be encouraged, apart from their private prayers:

- to participate in corporate worship at least weekly;
- to participate in the Eucharist at least once each month;

An average worshipper, attending weekly, should in a typical month:

- hear a balance of Old Testament and New Testament Scriptures, including a Gospel reading more often than not;
- encounter authorized prayers of penitence and the Lord's Prayer at most services;

---

14 Tarrant, *Worship and Freedom*, p. 26.

> • say or sing an authorized Creed or Affirmation of Faith
>   at least twice;
> • pray for the church and the world beyond their parish
>   at least twice.
>
> A visitor to the congregation should
>
> • be welcomed, comforted, inspired and challenged;
> • have the freedom to participate or not as they choose;
> • not be excluded from significant parts of the service
>   by the assumption that they are already familiar with
>   words, tunes, posture or actions.

We might not all agree with the detail of these suggested guidelines, but the idea of guidelines which focus on the liturgical diet of actual worshippers, rather than on the liturgical menu provided by the church, seems like a positive way forward.

Discipline

I hope that it will be clear from the above that what I am suggesting is not a complete free-for-all. This means that there still remains the question of ecclesiastical discipline – that is, what do you do when it goes wrong, when the 'Anglican' worship does not seem to connect in any way with Anglican tradition, and does not seem even to be heading in that direction? If there is to be accountability, then how are people held accountable and what happens when they are called to account and found wanting? Who can ask questions, who can challenge, who has the right to complain, and to whom?

These are important questions, but we would be no worse off than we are now. Already people are doing their own thing and breaking the rules that we have, and discipline has effectively broken down because the sanctions are so unclear and the process so complex and the result likely to be so unhelpful and self-defeating.

The difference would not be with the process of discipline, but with the basis on which discipline would be needed. The suggestions in this book are about moving from a juridical and legal framework to a relational one, focused on a relation of trust between local churches and their bishop and between one local church and another. Such relationships might not be present, or might break down. Still there would be the potential for problems. But at least the structures would allow for a different approach when there *was* a relationship of trust, and that must surely be a gain.

6

Conclusion

Summary – where have we got to?

This book began with the assessment that the current system of controlling worship in the Church of England is creaking and broken – though this has come about for good reasons, not bad ones. Despite all the right intentions, we've ended up with a system which is not fit for purpose in our current situation.

The current rule-based approach to worship has several unintended but detrimental consequences:

- It makes us focus on short-term questions of what is allowed rather than long-term strategy of how to make worship good.
- It overemphasizes liturgical text (which is controlled by rules), sidelining other aspects of worship performance, such as art, music and hymnody, and hindering a holistic and integrated approach to worship.
- It pushes creativity underground and stops it being shared openly, so good practice is harder to foster centrally (though it may thrive unofficially) and we are pushed further towards congregationalism.
- It therefore forces those who might be able to help (the Liturgical Commission, bishops) into the perceived role of 'enforcers' rather than enablers.
- It creates a culture of distrust rather than one of trust and de-skills clergy and other worship leaders.
- It makes us think that the tension between tradition and context is solved.

- It makes worship in pioneering and fresh expressions contexts particularly difficult to handle, putting leaders in difficult positions and potentially resulting in clumsy attempts to marry up missional approaches to worship with 'proper' content – especially when the bishop comes.

The solution is not to extend the boundaries even further (for this just makes the boundaries ever more complex, which helps no one in the long run). Instead, the suggested solution is to change the operating system from one based on rules and legality to one based on trust, loyalty and accountability – a centred set rather than a bounded one. This is not to suggest a free-for-all, but to make the level at which liturgical decision-making takes place more local, with historic and contemporary forms as benchmarks against which practice can be evaluated.

This entails letting go of the idea of liturgical conformity as a core part of what makes a church or an act of worship Anglican, and replacing it with concepts of relationship and accountability.

Implications – where do we go next?

There is a huge risk in suggesting such a wholesale paradigm shift in the way the Church of England sustains and nurtures its worship. One of the biggest risks is that the mere suggestion of it would be misunderstood – and it is important at this stage to stress again that making the choice of liturgical texts a local but accountable decision is *not* the same as saying 'ditch the Prayer Book and *Common Worship* everywhere'.

I think we must take that risk, and the reason is simple and has already been stated at the beginning of this book: a Church which says liturgy is very important, but has a liturgy which is too complicated for some to be able to get their heads round and feels too constrained for those who are doing some of the most interesting missional work and worship, is a Church that is in trouble.

Perhaps the bounded-set/centred-set models I have used are too crude. No doubt they are, because life is always more complicated than models. Well then, let us at least acknowledge that there are things to learn from using them, even if we conclude that a wholesale shift from one to the other is neither possible, nor desirable, nor even an accurate description of the situation we face.

The set theory is not the root of this book's argument. The basic argument is this: Can we move from control to trust in the way we regulate worship in the Church of England? Can we move from a situation in which central control feels like the norm, and freedom and flexibility the exception, to a situation in which trust, creativity, experiment (with accountability) is the norm, and central control is the exception? That shift would make for a much easier pattern of helping people to see where any boundaries were: imagine one relatively short book, which contained the texts or advice which was compulsory, and freedom to use other resources for everything else. In some ways, the reality would not be far from where we already are, but the presentation and 'feel' of it would be a world away.

This book is called *Beyond Common Worship*, because we need to think proactively beyond *Common Worship*, not let the problems pile up until we are forced into hasty, unthought-through and reactive responses. *Common Worship* in many ways and in many places is working well. But in many other places this is only the case because no one is asking the questions – it's not that CW is doing the job, it's that no one makes a fuss that lots of people are ignoring it. That is not a healthy way for a Church to function, especially one that sees its liturgy and worship as key to its mission and calling.

Many in the Church of England may be tired of liturgical revision after the complex and seemingly never-ending process of drafting, testing and authorizing *Common Worship*, but we need to grasp the liturgical nettle sooner rather than later – not primarily to tinker with *Common Worship* texts (though that may be necessary too, for other reasons), but to change the game, and recognize that we are in a new context which needs a new approach to worship in the Church of England.

Appendix 1

Some Examples of Worship Guidelines

Holy Communion

Default provision

The default provision for a service of Holy Communion should be one of the following:

- Order One or Order Two services of Holy Communion in *Common Worship*.
- A Service of the Word with Holy Communion in *Common Worship*.
- The order for Holy Communion in *The Book of Common Prayer*.

Other options

Local services of Holy Communion may vary from the above where there is good reason.

Good sources for other options include:

- The official liturgical resources of other Anglican Provinces.
- The official liturgical resources of Churches with whom we are in a Covenant relationship (i.e. the Methodist Church in Great Britain).

Decision-making and permission

Where a service of Holy Communion regularly deviates from official CW or BCP resources, the bishop should be consulted. The bishop may take advice and give direction about the services. The bishop should always be consulted about forms of Eucharistic Prayer and any other parts of the service which potentially have a significant impact on the understanding of Church of England doctrine.

In particular, the bishop will wish to be assured that the process of decision-making has been appropriately carried out and that the resulting service is consistent with the doctrinal and other norms of the Church of England.

Guidelines

A Holy Communion service should normally follow this outline shape:

- Gathering.
- Word.
- Sacrament.
- Dismissal.

A Holy Communion service should always include at least these elements:

- Corporate confession and assurance of forgiveness (normally using authorized forms).
- Readings from Scripture (normally two, one of which is from a Gospel).
- Preaching or other response to the Bible readings.
- Prayers of intercession and thanksgiving.
- A Eucharistic Prayer (either an authorized form or following the guidelines below).
- The Lord's Prayer.

- Distribution of the consecrated bread and wine to all present.
- Leftover bread and wine which has been consecrated is reverently consumed, either during or immediately after the service (except for any which is being reserved to be taken to the sick).

A Eucharistic Prayer should have the following basic structure and elements:

- Praise and thanksgiving to God for the words of creation, salvation and the sending of the Holy Spirit.
- An account of the Last Supper, and the interpretive words spoken by Jesus over the bread and wine.
- A calling down of the Holy Spirit (epiclesis) that the bread and wine 'might be for us the body and blood of Christ'.
- A formal remembering of Christ and his work (anamnesis).
- A concluding doxology.
- A final 'Amen' said by the people.

The Eucharistic Prayer would normally also include opportunity for the congregation to take part in the prayer, including some or all of the following:

- An opening dialogue between president and people.
- Praise for God's holiness ('Holy, holy, holy Lord . . .') based on Isaiah 6 (*Sanctus*), and possibly also the 'Blessed is he who comes in the name of the Lord' (*Benedictus qui venit*).
- Other responses during the prayer.
- Acclamations (such as, 'Christ has died, Christ is risen, Christ will come again').
- Sharing in an extended doxology and Amen.

Guidelines

Further guidelines for good practice for both the service and the Eucharistic Prayer can be found in *Methodist Worship Book*, pp. 221–2.

Lectionary (for Sundays or the equivalent main gathering of a congregation)

Default provision

The default lectionary for the main service in the church is the *Common Worship* Principal Service Lectionary or the lectionary from *The Book of Common Prayer*.

Where there is more than one service in a church on Sundays, the *Common Worship* Second Service Lectionary or the BCP lectionaries for Morning and Evening Prayer would make good alternatives.

Other options

Where there are good reasons, other lectionary provision can be used, including material devised locally.

A good source for lectionary material, as well as for inspiration and guidance, is *New Patterns for Worship*, Section C.

Decision-making and permission

Any decision to use local material rather than official lectionary material should be made jointly between the incumbent and PCC.

Decisions about what local material is used should involve clergy, Readers and others on any leadership or ministry team, and should be reported to the PCC.

Guidelines

Local churches should plan to base their Bible readings in public worship on either *Common Worship* or BCP material for at least part of the year, and this would normally include the main seasonal parts of the year (i.e. Lent and Eastertide, Advent, Christmas and the Epiphany season).

Where a church makes local choices about readings, they should ensure that over the course of a whole year, there is a good balance of biblical material read in public worship, including the Gospels, the rest of the New Testament, and the Old Testament (Hebrew Bible).

The norm should be for there to be at least two readings at the main Sunday service (or main gathering of the congregation), of which one would normally be a Gospel reading. Where the service includes Holy Communion, one of the readings should be a Gospel reading unless there is a very good reason for it not to be. Where a Gospel reading is omitted regularly, the bishop should be consulted for advice.

Appendix 2

Some Sample Canons, Applying the New Approach

What might the Canons look like if the ideas in this book were applied? What follows is not an attempt to provide fully thought-through legal provision, but to give a flavour of what rewritten Canons might seek to provide for.

Existing Canons of the Church of England (Seventh Edition)	Suggestions for revision (working text, not final proposals) [New or altered text is indicated by *italic*]
B 1 Of conformity of worship	**B 1 Of conformity of worship**
1. The following forms of service shall be authorized for use in the Church of England:	1. The following forms of service shall be authorized for use in the Church of England:
(a) the forms of service contained in *The Book of Common Prayer*;	[continues as in left hand column]
(b) the shortened forms of Morning and Evening Prayer which were set out in the Schedule to the Act of Uniformity Amendment Act 1872;	. . . approved by the General Synod.
(c) the form of service authorized by Royal Warrant for use upon	***B 1 A Of local forms of service*** *In addition to the forms of service indicated in Canon B 1 for use in the Church of England, the*

the anniversary of the day of the accession of the reigning Sovereign;

(d) any form of service approved under Canon B 2 subject to any amendments so approved, to the extent permitted by such approval;

(e) any form of service approved under Canon B 4 subject to any amendments so approved, to the extent permitted by such approval;

(f) any form of service authorized by the archbishops under Canon B 5A, to the extent permitted by such authorization.

2. Every minister shall use only the forms of service authorized by this Canon, except so far as he may exercise the discretion permitted by Canon B 5. It is the minister's responsibility to have a good understanding of the forms of service used and he shall endeavour to ensure that the worship offered glorifies God and edifies the people.

3. In this Canon the expression 'form of service' shall be construed as including –

(i) the prayers known as Collects;

diocesan bishop may approve a form of service for local use (for instance in a parish, cathedral or chaplaincy context) for a particular time.

Such a form of service shall only be approved if, in the opinion of the Ordinary, it is in both words and order reverent and seemly and neither contrary to, nor indicative of any departure from, the doctrine of the Church of England in any essential matter.

Such a form of service shall only be approved if it has been discussed and agreed between the minister having the cure of souls and the PCC (or equivalent).

Such forms shall be reviewed by the bishop at least every 5 years. In approving such a form of worship, the local church and the bishop shall have consideration for the ways it connects with existing authorized liturgy within the Church of England, and the implications for other Church of England churches in the vicinity.

In making a decision about local forms of service, the bishop shall have regard to relevant advice given by the Diocesan Liturgical Advisory Group (or equivalent) and

(ii) the lessons designated in any Table of Lessons;

(iii) any other matter to be used as part of a service;

(iv) any Table of rules for regulating a service;

(v) any Table of Holy Days which expression includes 'A Table of all the Feasts' in *The Book of Common Prayer* and such other Days as shall be included in any Table approved by the General Synod.

the Church of England Liturgical Commission.

B 1 B *Of hymns and songs used in services*

1. *Every minister having the cure of souls shall ensure that due regard is paid to the content of songs and hymns which are used during acts of worship, whether those songs or hymns are chosen by the minister concerned or by others.*

2. *All songs and hymns used in services in the Church of England should be neither contrary to, nor indicative of any departure from, the doctrine of the Church of England in any essential matter.*

Commentary:

The existing canon provides for worship which is approved for the whole Church of England. The suggested alteration would allow for approval to be given for forms of service to be used in particular localities (rather than a global permission) and for limited time frames. In that sense, it applies the principles which already exist for national liturgy and scales them down for local use and approval at diocesan level. In some ways it would also parallel the provisions which already exist in Canon B 2A for the bishop to approve the extension of the use of an alternative service for a particular parish after it has ceased to be authorized for the Church of England generally. (This provision was used to help parishes to make the move from ASB to CW.) It also draws on insights from the provision in Canon B 4.3 for the diocesan bishop to approve forms of service for diocesan use on particular occasions. Whereas that canon stresses that this should be for occasions for which there is no provision in the BCP, this alternative would allow for wider scope.

The suggested Canon B 1B extends the requirement for forms of service to conform to Church of England doctrine to songs and hymns. This would supplement the requirement already existing in Canon B 20.3 that music should be appropriate for the form of service and for the congregation, by stressing the importance of doctrinal content in songs and hymns.

B 5 Of the discretion of ministers in conduct of public prayer	B 5 Of the discretion of ministers in conduct of public prayer
1. The minister who is to conduct the service may in his discretion make and use variations which are not of substantial importance in any form of service authorized by Canon B 1 according to particular circumstances.	1. The minister who is to conduct the service may in his *or her* discretion make and use variations which are not of substantial importance in any form of service authorized by Canon B 1 according to particular circumstances.
2. The minister having the cure of souls may on occasions for which no provision is made in *The Book of Common Prayer* or by the General Synod under Canon B 2 or by the Convocations, archbishops, or Ordinary under Canon B 4 use forms of service considered suitable by him for those occasions and may permit another minister to use the said forms of service.	2. The minister having the cure of souls may *on particular occasions* use forms of service considered suitable by him *or her* for those occasions and may permit another minister to use the said forms of service. *Where such forms of service are expected to be used regularly, the minister having the cure of souls should seek*

3. All variations in forms of service and all forms of service used under this Canon shall be reverent and seemly and shall be neither contrary to, nor indicative of any departure from, the doctrine of the Church of England in any essential matter.

4. If any question is raised concerning the observance of the provisions of this Canon it may be referred to the bishop in order that he may give such pastoral guidance, advice or directions as he may think fit, but such reference shall be without prejudice to the matter in question being made the subject matter of proceedings under the Ecclesiastical Jurisdiction Measure 1963.

5. In this Canon the expression 'form of service' has the same meaning as in Canon B 1.

approval from the bishop as indicated under Canon B 1A.

3. All forms of service used under this Canon shall be reverent and seemly and shall be neither contrary to, nor indicative of any departure from, the doctrine of the Church of England in any essential matter.

4. If any question is raised concerning the observance of the provisions of this Canon it may be referred to the bishop in order that he *or she* may give such pastoral guidance, advice or directions as he *or she* may think fit, but such reference shall be without prejudice to the matter in question being made the subject matter of proceedings under the Ecclesiastical Jurisdiction Measure 1963.

5. In this Canon the expression 'form of service' has the same meaning as in Canon B 1.

Commentary:

The main suggested change here is to Canon B 5.2, where the provision for occasional use of a service is extended beyond occasions for which no provision is made in BCP or other authorized alternatives. This allows for local temporary or one-off discretion. For regular use, the suggestions outlined above in Canon B 1A would apply.

Canon B 5.3 is the balance to such freedom, requiring that any services used are consistent with Church of England doctrine. This would provide criteria for accountability.

B 8 Of the vesture of ordained and authorized ministers during the time of divine service	B 8 Of the vesture of ordained and authorized ministers during the time of divine service
1. The Church of England does not attach any particular doctrinal significance to the diversities of vesture permitted by this Canon, and the vesture worn by the minister in accordance with the provision of this Canon is not to be understood as implying any doctrines other than those now contained in the formularies of the Church of England.	1. *The Church of England does not attach any particular doctrinal significance to the diversities of vesture in use, and the vesture worn by the minister is not to be understood as implying any doctrines other than those now contained in the formularies of the Church of England.*
2. Notwithstanding the provisions of this Canon no minister shall change the form of vesture in use in the church or chapel in which he officiates unless he has ascertained by consultation with the parochial church council that such changes will be acceptable: Provided always that in case of disagreement the minister shall refer the matter to the bishop of the diocese, whose direction shall be obeyed.	2. Notwithstanding the provisions of this Canon no minister shall change the form of vesture in use in the church or chapel in which he *or she* officiates unless he *or she* has ascertained by consultation with the parochial church council that such changes will be acceptable *and are being made for good reasons*: Provided always that in case of disagreement the minister shall refer the matter to the bishop of the diocese, whose direction shall be obeyed.

3. At the Holy Communion the presiding minister shall wear either a surplice or alb with scarf or stole. When a stole is worn other customary vestments may be added. The epistoler and gospeller (if any) may wear surplice or alb to which other customary vestments may be added.

4. At Morning and Evening Prayer on Sundays the minister shall normally wear a surplice or alb with scarf or stole.

5. At the Occasional Offices the minister shall wear a surplice or alb with scarf or stole.

3. At the Holy Communion it will be particularly important to ensure that it is clear to those present that the presiding minister is a priest or bishop, whether through vesture or in other ways.

4. At pastoral services (the Occasional Offices) the minister shall have due regard, when choosing vesture, to the needs and expectations of those for whom the service is being provided.

Commentary:

Here the responsibility for deciding on vesture is shifted clearly to the local church, but with the proviso that such decisions shall not belong to the minister alone, but should be the subject of discussion, and that changes should be for good reason and not at the whim of the minister. For lengthier discussion of the issues at stake here, see Andrew Atherstone, *Clergy Robes and Mission Priorities*, Grove Worship Series 197, Cambridge: Grove Books, 2008.

Select Bibliography

General

Will Adam, *Legal Flexibility and the Mission of the Church: Dispensation and Economy in Ecclesiastical Law*, Farnham: Ashgate, 2011.

Andrew Atherstone, *Clergy Robes and Mission Priorities*, Grove Worship Series 197, Cambridge: Grove Books, 2008.

Jonny Baker and Dean Ayres, *Making Communion: Grace Pocket Liturgies*, Proost – www.proost.co.uk, 2012.

Colin Buchanan (ed.), *Michael Vasey, Liturgist and Friend*, Cambridge: Grove Books, 1999.

Andrew Chandler and David Hein, *Archbishop Fisher, 1945–1961: Church, State and World*, Farnham: Ashgate, 2012.

Adrian Chatfield, 'Form and Freedom: Creating Pioneering Worship', in Dave Male (ed.), *Pioneers 4 Life: Explorations in Theology and Wisdom*, Abingdon: BRF, 2011, pp. 115–26.

Church of England, *Ecumenical Relations: Canons B43 & B44 – Code of Practice* (1989 with 1997 supplements), London: General Synod, 1989, 1997.

Church of England: Liturgical Commission, *Making Women Visible: The Use of Inclusive Language with the ASB* (GS 859), London: Church House Publishing, 1989.

Church of England: Liturgical Commission, *Patterns for Worship* (GS 898), London: Church House Publishing, 1989.

Church of England: Liturgical Commission, *The Worship of the Church as it Approaches the Third Millennium* (GS Misc 364), London: Church House Publishing, 1991.

Church of England: *Mission-shaped Church: Church Planting and Fresh Expressions of Church in a Changing Context* (GS1523), London: Church House Publishing, 2004.

Church of England: Liturgical Commission, *Transforming Worship: Living the New Creation* (GS1651), London: General Synod of the Church of England, 2007.

Graham Cray, 'Common Worship – Common Mission', *Faith and Worship* 71 (Trinity 2012), pp. 7–16.

Steven, Croft (ed.), *The Future of the Parish System: Shaping the Church of England for the 21st Century*, London: Church House Publishing, 2006.

Steven Croft (ed.), *Mission-shaped Questions: Defining Issues for Today's Church*, London: Church House Publishing, 2008.

Mark Earey, *Worship Audit: Making Good Worship Better*, Grove Worship Series 133, Nottingham: Grove Books, 1995.

Mark Earey, *Producing Your Own Orders of Service*, London: Church House Publishing, 2000.

Mark Earey, *Finding Your Way Around Common Worship: A Simple Guide*, London: Church House Publishing, 2011.

David Gitari (ed.), *Anglican Liturgical Inculturation in Africa: The Kanamai Statement 'African Culture and Anglican Liturgy'*, Alcuin/GROW Joint Liturgical Study 28, Nottingham: Grove Books, 1994.

Donald Gray, *The 1927–28 Prayer Book Crisis (1)*, Alcuin/GROW Joint Liturgical Studies 60, Norwich: Canterbury Press, 2005.

David Hebblethwaite, *Liturgical Revision in the Church of England 1984–2004: The Working of the Liturgical Commission*, Alcuin/GROW Joint Liturgical Studies 57, Cambridge: Grove Books, 2004.

Paul G. Hiebert, *Anthropological Reflections on Mission Issues*, Grand Rapids: Baker Books, 1994.

David R. Holeton (ed.), *Liturgical Inculturation in the Anglican Communion*, Alcuin/GROW Joint Liturgical Study 15, Nottingham: Grove Books, 1990.

Christopher Irvine (ed.), *Anglican Liturgical Identity: Papers from the Prague Meeting of the International Anglican Liturgical Consultation*, Alcuin/GROW Joint Liturgical Studies 65, Norwich: Canterbury Press, 2008.

Christopher Irvine and Anders Bergquist, 'Thinking about Liturgy', *Anaphora* 5:2 (2011), pp. 45–56.

R. C. D. Jasper, *The Development of the Anglican Liturgy 1662–1980*, London: SPCK, 1989.

David Kennedy, *Understanding Anglican Worship: A Parish Study Guide*, Grove Worship Series 130, Nottingham: Grove Books, 1994.

Trevor Lloyd (comp.), *The Future of Anglican Worship*, Grove Worship Series 100, Nottingham: Grove Books, 1987.

Peter Moger, *Crafting Common Worship: A Practical, Creative Guide to What's Possible*, London: Church House Publishing, 2009.

Michael Moynagh, *Church for Every Context: An Introduction to Theology and Practice*, London: SCM Press, 2012.

Stuart Murray, *Church after Christendom*, Milton Keynes: Paternoster Press, 2004.

Nicholas Papadopulos (ed.), *God's Transforming Work: Celebrating Ten Years of Common Worship,* London: SPCK, 2011.

Michael Perham (ed.), *The Renewal of Common Prayer: Unity and Diversity in Church of England Worship* (GS Misc 412), London: Church House Publishing/SPCK, 1993.

Michael Perham (ed.), *Towards Liturgy 2000: Preparing for the Revision of the Alternative Service Book*, London: SPCK/Alcuin Club, 1989.

Michael Perham, 'Liturgical Revision 1981–2000', in Paul Bradshaw (ed.), *A Companion to Common Worship, Volume 1*, London: SPCK, 2001.

Royal Commission on Ecclesiastical Discipline, *Report of the Royal Commission on Ecclesiastical Discipline*, London: HMSO, 1906.

John Scrivener, 'Paradoxes of "Inculturation"', *Faith and Worship* 71 (Trinity 2012), pp. 3–6.

Kenneth Stevenson and Bryan Spinks (eds), *The Identity of Anglican Worship*, London: Mowbray, 1991.

Stephen Sykes, 'Ritual and the Sacrament of the Word', in David Brown and Ann Loades (eds), *Christ: The Sacramental Word*, London: SPCK, 1996, pp. 157–67.

Ian Tarrant, *Worship and Freedom in the Church of England: Exploring the Boundaries*, Grove Worship Series 210, Cambridge: Grove Books, 2012.

Angela Tilby, 'What Questions Does Catholic Ecclesiology Pose for Fresh Expressions?', in Steven Croft (ed.), *Mission-Shaped Questions: Defining Issues for Today's Church*, London: Church House Publishing, 2008, pp. 78–89.

Phillip Tovey, *Mapping Common Worship: Mind Maps to Find Your Way Round All the Volumes of Common Worship*, Grove Worship Series 195, Cambridge: Grove Books, 2008.

Michael Vasey, 'Modern Ordinands and the *Book of Common Prayer*', in Margot Johnson (ed.), *Thomas Cranmer: Essays in Commemoration of the 500th Anniversary of his Birth*, Durham: Turnstone Ventures, 1990, pp. 273–90.

Liturgical texts

Church of England, *The Book of Common Prayer*, 1662.

Church of England, *The Alternative Service Book 1980*, London: Mowbray/Oxford: Oxford University Press, 1980.

Church of England, *Ministry to the Sick: Authorized Alternative Services*, Cambridge: Cambridge University Press/Colchester: William Clowes/Oxford: A. R. Mowbray & Co./Oxford: Oxford University Press/London: SPCK, 1983.

Church of England, *Lent, Holy Week, Easter: Services and Prayers*, London: Church House Publishing/Cambridge: Cambridge University Press/London: SPCK, 1986.

Church of England, *Promise of His Glory: Services and Prayers for the Season from All Saints to Candlemas*, London: Church House Publishing/Mowbray, 1991.

Church of England, *A Service of the Word and Affirmations of Faith, Authorized for use in the Church of England*, London: Church House Publishing, 1994.

Church of England, *Patterns for Worship*, London: Church House Publishing, 1995.

Church of England, *Common Worship: Services and Prayers for the Church of England*, London: Church House Publishing, 2000.

Church of England, *Common Worship: Daily Prayer*, London: Church House Publishing, 2005.

Church of England, *Common Worship: Pastoral Services*, London: Church House Publishing, 2005.

Church of England, *Common Worship: Christian Initiation*, London: Church House Publishing, 2006.

Methodist Church, *Methodist Worship Book*, Peterborough: Methodist Publishing House, 1999.

Michael Perham (comp.), *Enriching the Christian Year*, London: SPCK/Alcuin Club, 1993.

Society of Saint Francis, *Celebrating Common Prayer: A Version of the Daily Office SSF*, London: Mowbray, 1992.

Index